Plato's *Seventh Letter*

Plato's *Seventh Letter*

Translation and Commentary by
JAMES M. REDFIELD

Edited by Schuyler Curriden

HACKETT PUBLISHING COMPANY
INDIANAPOLIS

Copyright © 2026 by Hackett Publishing Company, Inc.

All rights reserved
Printed in the United States of America

29 28 27 26   1 2 3 4 5 6 7

For further information, please address
   Hackett Publishing Company, Inc.
   P.O. Box 44937
   Indianapolis, Indiana 46244-0937

   www.hackettpublishing.com

Hackett Publishing Company, Inc. | Independent | Employee Owned

Cover design by Listenberger Design & Associates
Interior design by E. L. Wilson
Composition by Aptara, Inc.

Cataloging-in-Publication data can be accessed via the Library of Congress Online Catalog. Library of Congress Control Number: 2025942565

ISBN-13: 978-1-64792-256-6 (pbk.)
ISBN-13: 978-1-64792-260-3 (PDF ebook)
ISBN-13: 978-1-64792-261-0 (epub)

The paper used in this publication meets the minimum requirements of American National Standard for Information Sciences—Permanence of Paper for Printed Library Materials, ANSI Z39.48–1984.

CONTENTS

Introduction	vii
Note on Text and Translation	xvi
Acknowledgments	xvii
Plato's *Seventh Letter*	1
Commentary	29
Appendix: A Translation of Selections from Plutarch's *Life of Dion*	93
Bibliography	103

INTRODUCTION

This book is intended to introduce Plato's *Seventh Letter* to a wider audience. I have noticed that many people interested in Plato have never heard of Plato's *Seventh Letter*, that those who have heard of it have seldom read it, and that those who have read it have most often been puzzled by what to make of it. I shall begin by addressing myself to the first group with a brief description of the *Seventh Letter* (hereinafter simply the *Letter*).

The *Letter* is a text about the size of one book of the *Republic*. It is addressed by Plato to the Friends of Dion and purports to advise them as to their plans and aims after the death of Dion, which occurred in the course of the civil conflict at Syracuse during a period when the tyrant Dionysius the Younger was out of power and in exile. This violence at Syracuse was the indirect result of Plato's effort, in cooperation with Dion, to convert the young tyrant to philosophy and thus bring peace and happiness to Sicily.

The actual advice to Dion's friends takes up only a small part of the *Letter*; there is also much about politics at Syracuse, about Plato's involvement in that and his evolving attitude toward it, about his relations with Dion, and also about Plato's understanding of the method and aims of his kind of philosophy.[1]

The text was composed in something very like Plato's late literary style. It is generally agreed to date to the late fourth century BCE, although a few scholars place it early in the third. It is an important source for our understanding of the politics of Syracuse and Plato's Academy during those years. (Those who do not know much about the Academy may be reassured to learn that very little is known. It follows that every scrap of evidence is valuable.[2])

---

1. See, however, Knab's (2006, 44–50) argument that the entirety of the letter can be understood as contributing to the aim of bringing the friends of Dion to "die eigene Verständnisebene," so that they can understand the counsel he gives in the relatively brief *sumboulē*.
2. See Lombardini (2023, 7–18) for a discussion of the scholarly debates around the Academy with particular relevance to the narrative of the *Letter*.

The seventh is one of thirteen letters that have come down to us as part of the corpus of Plato's writings. The thirty-five dialogues (some of which are now generally thought not to be by Plato) were arranged by Thrasyllus in the first century CE into groups of four, with the letters filling out the last tetralogy. (After the letters is a curious text called *Definitions* and six dialogues that are classified as spurious.) The seventh is much the longest of the letters (longer than the other twelve put together) and the most interesting.

When I mention this document to people who have heard of it, the first question is usually "Do you think it is authentic?" They are not asking if it is a modern forgery; the question of authenticity is generally asked in the context of an assumption that it was composed during Plato's lifetime or shortly after his death. They want to know if these are Plato's authentic words rather than those of someone speaking for him. There is almost always a silent corollary: "If it is not, what reason is there to pay any attention to it?" That is a question with answers. Doing history, it is unwise to discard documents. The *Letter*, whatever it is, is authentically that. We have a text of uncertain authorship, not securely dated, but none the less worthy of study. If it is not by Plato, it might nevertheless tell some truth about him, his situation, and his work—and if it is by Plato, it is not necessarily completely truthful. Indeed we shall see that in some respects, the *Letter* falsifies the story, if only by excluding certain facts.

I believe the *Letter* is by Plato, and I shall say why. I shall also have a few things to say about the arguments on the other side. I do not find any of these arguments particularly strong; nevertheless, their conclusion may be right. Therefore it follows that we need to read the *Letter* twice, once on the assumption that these are Plato's words and that he had his own reasons for writing them, and then on the assumption that they are the words of someone who, for whatever reason, is speaking for Plato. In what follows, I shall speak of the author simply as "Plato." (This actually is, at worst, no more deceptive than saying "Socrates says," meaning the character in Plato or Xenophon.) In the conclusion, I shall briefly return to the alternative hypothesis and consider the difference it makes.

I find the *Letter* to be something like Abelard's *Story of My Misfortunes* or Wilde's *De Profundis*: it is a first-person account by someone who has made a terrible mistake—made it more than once, actually—and who takes responsibility but wants us to know that he was not really at fault, or not as much as others.³ The key point, for me, is that there is nothing else like this in classical Greek. In the fourth century, we have a number of first-person accounts—by Xenophon, Isocrates, and Demosthenes; also, Aristophanes speaks in his own person in some of his plays—but none of those are like this. Theirs are stories of clear motives, of their failures or more often, their successes, and occasionally of damage done to them by others. Plato takes us into the subjective space where the errors were made, telling us of his conflicted motives and the inner debate they generated. As far as our information goes, writing like this was completely original with this author. So, we should have to hypothesize the existence of an exceptionally creative author about whose talent we otherwise know nothing. It is surely a simpler hypothesis to attribute the *Letter* to Plato, whom we know to have had such gifts.⁴ Occam's razor can be applied.

I do not expect this argument to end the dispute about the *Letter*'s authorship. It has been going on for centuries and will probably never be settled. A crowd of scholars has written for and against.⁵ The most thoughtful and thorough defense of authenticity known to me is Pasquali's (1938), point by point refuted by Maddalena (1948); the refutation was, in turn,

---

3. Brisson (1993, sec.32) characterizes it in the following manner: "La Lettre VII est donc bien une autobiographie, mais une autobiographie qui se veut une apologie, une apologie de Platon par lui-même et, par la même occasion, une apologie de celui qui fut son disciple, Dion."
4. Pappas and Momigliano, cited in Helfer (2023, 17), voice similar arguments.
5. Sanders (2008, 1n1) lists sixteen items against authenticity and fifty-one in favor; he himself is firmly against it. Since this accounting, notable arguments against authenticity include Burnyeat and Frede's 2015 book, discussed below; and Irwin (2009), who suggests Speusippus may have written the *Letter*. Arguments for authenticity include Liatsi (2008), who develops an extensive interpretation of the "philosophical digression," which she calls the "erkenntnistheoretischer Teil," on the assumption of authenticity; Notomi (2019), on the basis of a comparison with the history of fourth-century letter-writing; Politis (2020), who develops a reading of the "philosophical digression" compatible with authenticity; Helfer (2023), who goes so far as to revive the "literary unity thesis" of Dornseiff (1934), maintaining the authenticity of all thirteen letters; and Waterfield's biography of Plato takes the *Letter* to be authentic and reliable as a historical source, though he strangely claims that "scholarly consensus is that none of the Letters are genuine" and only "a significant minority of scholars [. . .] believe that some of the letters are genuine" (2023, xxxi).

carefully refuted by Isnardi Parente (1970)—with extensive reference to Pasquali. A lot turns on what one considers to be relevant evidence.

Ludwig Edelstein wrote a substantial and carefully written monograph (1966) to deny the *Letter*'s authenticity. He has two main arguments: first, that the political program for Syracuse set forth in the *Letter* is inconsistent with the *Republic*; second, that the program for Sicily is that of Timoleon and, therefore, must have been composed after Timoleon's expedition. To these, I would respond that, first, the *Republic* does not in any ordinary sense set forth a political program; what is called within the dialogue "the *politeia*," the ideal state, is a thought experiment intended for the education of Glaucon—and to a lesser extent for Adeimantus. As such, it is throughout implicitly about the constitution of the soul, as is explicitly the case in the concluding tenth book. As to the second, it seems to me that the needs of Greek Sicily were sufficiently obvious long before Timoleon; the question was how to meet them. Plato seems to have imagined that philosophy would be the solution. He failed, as did Dion when he turned to the use of force. Eventually Timoleon arrived with sufficient forces and detachment from local political interests to enforce a settlement, which gave Syracuse sixty years of constitutional government until the next tyrant.

The most recurrent disqualification of the *Letter* on the basis of a comparison with Plato's works has to do with the so-called "philosophical digression" (342a–343b). Various writers find various ways to tell us that this passage is un-Platonic because it is not consistent with Plato's Theory of Ideas (never called a "theory" in the *Dialogues*, but a "way of speaking"). Here again it seems to be assumed that a careful reading of the *Dialogues* will give us a clear understanding of Plato's own metaphysics, so we can then argue that the digression differs from that. However, such passages as the analogy of the divided line in *Republic* VI and the myth of the soul in the *Phaedrus* are not presented as Platonic theories but as Socratic images. I know of no cogent explanation as to why, if these are Plato's views, he presented them in this indirect way.

Furthermore, the digression is not inserted in the *Letter* as a metaphysical explanation but to clarify the writer's assertion that his philosophy "cannot be put into words like other objects of study" (341c) because of the "weakness of language" (342e). It is to be expected that anyone trying to explain the inexplicable should express himself somewhat awkwardly; the passage does help us understand why Plato did not write treatises (as other Socratics, in fact, did). There is a lot of discomfort in the *Letter*—throughout; Plato evidently was only comfortable in print when speaking with other voices.

To make a long story short, I would assert rejecting the *Letter* on the grounds that it is un-Platonic tends to ignore the point that if it is by Plato, writing it was in itself an un-Platonic thing to do. Plato, however, was not required to be Platonic all the time. Furthermore, it is, in my view, dangerous to assume that we already understand what Plato meant and what he was about and that because this *Letter* presents something different from that understanding, it is, therefore, not by him.[6] The assumption may lose us something important, namely, a chance to see him differently.

The important question is not really about authorship, because someone other than Plato might be conveying a valid account of Plato's enterprise in this form. Those who reject the *Letter* as not by Plato generally take this to imply that it is not worth reading because it is not infused with something they recognize as Platonic philosophy. The *Letter*, I think, is most interesting when it puts "Platonic philosophy" into question.

This issue is sharply raised by the most recent attack on the *Letter*'s authenticity: *The Pseudo-Platonic Seventh Letter* by Myles Burnyeat and Michael Frede (2015). These texts (Frede's was posthumously reconstructed from his seminar notes; Burnyeat's was freshly composed) share a common position: they know what a philosopher is; the *Letter* was clearly not composed by one; therefore the *Letter* is not by Plato. This is not a syllogism, nor do they think of an alternative solution: that Plato was not a philosopher as they understand the term.

Burnyeat's understanding of "philosophy" is foregrounded, for example, in his statement that the author of the philosophical digression "is philosophically incompetent" and, therefore (it is taken for granted that this follows), not Plato. He supports this statement with a careful analysis of the "philosophical digression," fully displaying Burnyeat's own competence.

---

6. Reale's criticism of doubters of the *Seventh Letter*'s inauthenticity proceeds along similar lines, though in defense of a Tübinger School interpretation: "Die These von der Inauthentizität des *7. Briefes* basiert auf einem regelrechten Zirkelschluß: Man lehnt die Authentizität dieser Schrift deswegen ab, weil man nicht akzeptiert, was sie über das Schriftliche sagt, da dies nicht in das hermeneutische Paradigma paßt, dem man Folge leistet" (Reale 1993, 105).

He goes on to a fine account of the *Letter*'s literary structure and qualities—again with the implication that Plato could not have written thus. The subjectivity, the innerness of the narrative he repeatedly calls "psychodrama"—with this pejorative term suggesting that such conflicting emotions could not be felt, or at least would not be published, by a philosopher. I would respond that we do not have good evidence for Plato's competence as a philosopher in Burnyeat's sense (although some of his later work tends in that direction). However, we have plenty of evidence for Plato's gifts as an imaginative writer. That, as I said, is for me the main reason to believe that the *Letter* is by Plato.

Frede's understanding of "philosophy" is best displayed in his discussion of Dion's qualifications as a philosopher/ruler. He concludes: "Nothing in the evidence . . . even suggests . . . that Dion subjected himself to a serious course of study. . . . No source ever attributes any philosophical view or position to Dion" (Burnyeat and Frede 2015, 63). But I would suggest that for Plato philosophy is not a matter of views or positions—or competence; it is rather a matter of commitment, what Hellenistic Greek called a *hairesis*, the choice to join a school or brand of philosophy. Of course, in the Platonic world, this commitment is to an *askēsis*, a way of life that involves certain kinds of self-denial and also certain *mathēmata*, studies that train the mind as it engages in philosophical discourse. The readiness to accept that *askēsis* is precisely the "test" described in the *Letter* (340b–341a). Evidently Dion passed that test when he and Plato first met; however, the evidence we have—from the *Letter* and other sources—must make us doubt the degree to which he was faithful to that commitment. There is a question as to why Plato was so tolerant of Dion's shortcomings, but that question does not touch on the authenticity of the *Letter*.

There is one place in the ancient literature where Dion speaks of the Academy. When Dion's friends urged him not to spare his enemies, Plutarch (*Dion* 47) tells us that he responded:

> Other generals have mainly trained themselves in arms and war, but I in my long time in the Academy kept up the practice of overcoming anger and envy and every kind of contention. The proof of this is not in moderation to one's friends and allies, but rather when one is quick to pardon unfair treatment, and be gentle to wrongdoers. I would wish to be seen overcoming Heracleides [leader of the opposition to Dion at Syracuse] not so much by power and policy, but by decency and fairness.

> True superiority is there. Military success, even if no man can dispute it with you, always owes something to the fortunes of war. If Heracleides was unfaithful and wicked out of envy, not for that should Dion corrupt his own virtue out of anger. To punish in revenge is held in law to be more just than striking the first blow, but both proceed from the same weakness in our nature. Human vice, however harsh it may be, is not so altogether savage and sour that it cannot be converted to grace by repeated good treatment.

That Plutarch quotes this does not, of course, mean that Dion was sincere or even authentically said it—although Timonides might well have heard and recorded something like this. We can say, however, that someone thought these remarks a plausible result of time spent in Plato's Academy. Frede (quoted above) clearly did not think any of this constituted a "philosophical view or position."

Frede makes other points against the *Letter*. He reminds us that writing letters to be attributed to famous persons was a favorite literary exercise in antiquity. He does admit that we recognize a few of these ancient letters as authentic. Frede says, however, that Plato's letters "antedate any clearly authentic letters of philosophers by sixty or seventy years" (Burnyeat and Frede 2015, 11). He is able to say this because he classifies Isocrates's letters—"at least some of which are genuine"—as "rhetoricians' or orators' letters" (4). Isocrates, however, frequently calls his own activity "philosophy." In one place, he says that the point of philosophy is "to know how to foresee the advantageous" (*Speeches* 1.40). This is hardly consistent with Socrates in the *Gorgias*—it sounds more like Callicles—but in the fourth century BCE, philosophy was a highly contested term.

Isocrates's antipathy to the Academy (especially in *Against the Sophists*) evidently turns on his implicit rejection of the Academy's assertion of the difference between knowledge and opinion. Opinion is all there is, he seems to say; deal with it. This is a philosophical position. If Isocrates had written out his principles instead of taking them for granted, they might have looked much like those of, say, Richard Rorty. Rorty says somewhere, "If you ask a pragmatist, 'What is truth?' he changes the subject."

We know what Isocrates thought because he tells us. If we want to know what Plato thought of philosophy, we need to look at his texts. However, Plato—as we well know—did not appear in his own texts either as a character or as the narrator. Furthermore, his chief protagonist, Socrates, is written as a master ironist who does not necessarily exactly agree with what he himself is saying. The only place—if at all—where Plato speaks in his own voice is in the letters. In the last chapter, we shall return to considering how this atypical first-person voice could affect our understanding of Plato's work. The best reason to study this text, in my view, is that it can open before us a fresh understanding of the relation between Plato's *Dialogues* and his philosophy.

This little book consists of a text—in my translation—and an extended comment on it. The comment is not intended as a contribution to philosophy but, at best, as a contribution to the history of philosophy. The modern literature on the *Letter* has not, on the whole, made much of it as a historical source.[7] The two best historical treatments known to me are in German: Berve (1957) and von Fritz (1968). (The latter incorporates, through reference and commentary, a great part of Berve.)

A historical treatment requires placing the text in context; here, we rely on the accounts we have of events before, during, and after Plato's visits to Syracuse, primarily in Plutarch's *Dion* but also in Diodorus Siculus and Cornelius Nepos. All three of these authors, of course, wrote centuries later, but they had access to earlier accounts now lost to us. Some of these were by actual participants and, therefore, eyewitnesses.[8] Philistus, a leading, perhaps the leading, advisor and minister to the Syracusan tyrants, both father and son and consistently an adversary to Dion, wrote histories admired in antiquity as Thucydidean. He is credited with two books—which may in effect have been parts of one book: a history of Sicily which picked up where Antiochus left off, and another covering the career of Dionysius the Elder. This latter must have been an important source for Dion's earlier political career. Then (Diodorus Siculus tells us—15.89.2), he wrote a brief history of the first five years of the tyranny of the younger Dionysius. This included the period of Plato's first attempt to educate

---

[7]. Exceptions include: Brunt (1993); Westlake (1994); the edited volume *Plato at Syracuse* (2019), particularly pp. 77–126; Waterfield (2023); and Romm's (2025) excellent treatment of the historical material, which covers some of the same ground as my own and unfortunately appeared too late for me to make use of.

[8]. For an account of the ancient historians who wrote on Dion, see Berve (1956, 748–57). See also Schneider (2019, esp. 108–10), for an account of the relationship between Plutarch, Diodorus, Nepos, and their sources.

Dionysius, but there is actually no evidence that he ever mentioned Plato. He might have thought him irrelevant to a history concerned with war and politics. Plutarch, or at least one of his sources, seems to have this book since there is one mention in Plutarch's narrative of a fact that should have been known only to Philistus and the tyrant himself.

Then there was Timonides of Leucas, an Academic who accompanied Dion on his expedition to conquer Syracuse and wrote one or more letters to Plato's nephew Speusippus describing the events. His attitude to Dion, so far as we can reconstruct it, was (predictably) uniformly favorable.

We can thus identify two major sources for events before Plato's visits to Dionysius the Younger and for events following those visits: Dion's victories in Syracuse and his death. For the period of Plato's visits, we have no contemporary source except Plato—or perhaps we should include Athanis of Syracuse, who, we are told, completed the *History* of Philistus. Unfortunately, no fragment of Athanis survives. He has, however, been plausibly identified as the source of Cornelius Nepos's relatively unsympathetic account of Dion's final period in Syracuse leading up to his death.

Plutarch and Diodorus may well have had access to the eyewitness texts, but they no doubt often worked from intermediate historians, principally Timaeus and Ephorus. Plutarch evidently relied mainly on Timaeus, while Diodorus mainly relied on Ephorus. Diodorus does not seem to have had the *Letter*; he says nothing about Plato's interactions with Dionysius the Younger, but he does have a good deal to say about Dion. Plutarch wrote the *Life of Dion*, but also finds much to say about Plato and draws extensively on the *Letter*. The *Letter* fits smoothly into the accounts given by these later writers; for von Fritz this is the chief proof of the *Letter*'s authenticity. Furthermore, he notes that the *Letter* provides explanations of a number of events which, while independently attested, are otherwise mysterious.

Here, I approach the text with a historian's questions: What is the story it tells? How truthful is it? How does it fit in with what else we know or think we know? What motivated its composition?

My suggestion to the reader is this: read the *Letter* first—in Greek if you can, or in translation, mine or another's. Then read my comment. Then read the *Letter* again and see if your sense of it has changed. My intention here is not to enforce conclusions but to open a discussion.

NOTE ON TEXT AND TRANSLATION

The basis for this volume's translation of Plato's *Seventh Letter* is John Burnet's 1907 text in the fifth volume of the Oxford Classical Texts edition of Plato's works. The Souilhé edition, which incorporates a limited number of variant readings from older manuscripts not included in the Burnet text, was also consulted; however, the variants were not deemed to bear upon the sense. The basis for this volume's translation of selections from Plutarch's *Life of Dion* is the Greek text provided by Porter's edition of 1918. The selections were based on direct relevance to the relationship between Plato and Dion. All translations of other ancient Greek material are by Redfield; their textual bases are indicated in the bibliography. All citations of Plato are to *Platonis Opera*. The aim of these translations is to render Plato and Plutarch into readable English while retaining the philosophical and stylistic rigor of the original.

ACKNOWLEDGMENTS

Schuyler Curriden appears on the title page for good reason. His work as an editor was invaluable in the completion of this manuscript: we have been in continuous correspondence in order to approach a publishable condition, which could not have been achieved without his considerable energy and expertise.

Special thanks are owed to Glenn Most for suggesting Hackett as an appropriate publisher and opening a conversation with them. I have been fortunate to learn much from Glenn over the years as my colleague on the Committee on Social Thought, and I hope this volume will continue our dialogue in a new form.

I would also like to thank Ewa Atanassow, a friend and collaborator whose invitation to lecture on Plato at Bard College Berlin helped me to articulate some ideas in the commentary over a long and memorable conversation in the garden thereafter.

After a doctoral dissertation that I suppressed, I have been trying to write a book on Plato for sixty-five years. This small book is the first that I could finish and will be the only one. It is no great mystery why I had to try so long. Plato is extraordinarily difficult, in part because he is never really writing about himself. Perhaps I could only write a book on the *Seventh Letter* because it is the exception, and even here, Plato is evidently writing about Dion. Then again, perhaps it is impossible to write an autobiography that is not about someone else.

PLATO'S
SEVENTH LETTER

Plato to Dion's relatives and companions: may you prosper

You wrote me that I should consider your policy the same as Dion's, and then you call upon me to join you, so far as I may be able, in act and speech. For my part, if you have the same views and intentions he had, I agree to join; otherwise I'll have to think about it quite a while. As to his policy and intentions, without guesswork but from clear knowledge I can speak. When I first came to Syracuse—I was about forty—Dion was of the age Hipparinus is now,[1] and the view he had at that time he had all his life: that the people of Syracuse should be free and be governed by the best laws. So it would not be amazing if some god had made Hipparinus of the same opinion in his views of the regime. How these views came to be is something fit for the ear of a young person—or one not so young—so I will try to tell you the whole story. There could be no better moment.

*   *   *

---

1. Which is to say, he is twenty-one. Plato came to Syracuse for the first time in 388 BCE. Some have thought that the Hipparinus mentioned here was Dion's son (Hipparinus was the name of Dion's father, and boys were often named for their grandfathers), but the Hipparinus meant is almost certainly the child of Dion's sister Aristomache and Dionysius the Elder. He must be one of the "nephews" (328a) mentioned as already recruited to his party by Dion when he first invited Plato to return to Sicily; this Hipparinus is known to have taken the leadership of Dion's party after Dion's death. For an alternative account of the dispute, see Helfer's (2023) note ad loc.

When I was a young man I felt as most of us[2] did: I thought that as soon as I came of age, I would immediately go into public life. It so happened that my political situation developed as follows: there was a revolution from the then widely derided constitution, and by this revolution, fifty-one men took charge of the government, Eleven in the city and Ten in the Piraeus—these two groups were concerned with the market and urban administration—while Thirty held absolute power over everything. Some of these were actually relatives[3] and acquaintances of mine, and so they immediately invited me to join, as fit work for me. It was no wonder what I felt, allowing for my youth: I thought they were going to administer the city, leading it away from injustice into some just way, and so I paid close attention to see what they would do. But what I saw was these men in no time making the previous regime by comparison look golden—in particular they sent for my older friend Socrates, whom I would not be ashamed to call the most just man of the time, and sent him with others after one of the citizens[4] to bring him in for execution in order that Socrates be implicated, willy-nilly, in their business. He would not consent, but was ready for any risk rather than get involved in their unholy acts—when I saw all this and some other pretty significant events, I was disgusted and recoiled from the vices of that time.

Not much later the Thirty fell and their whole regime with them; so once again—more slowly, it is true—I felt the urge for public affairs and politics. In the disorder of that time, a number of things happened which might well excite disgust, and it would have been no wonder if people had taken more revenge against their enemies in the course of the transfer of power. Actually the returned exiles acted pretty decently. However by some chance, certain powerful people brought this Socrates, our companion, into court, bringing against him a most impious charge

---

2. The Greek says, literally, "many people"—but Plato is clearly thinking of people like himself born into the political class.

3. Plato's relatives known to have been part of this regime are Critias, Plato's first cousin once removed and the leading member of the Thirty, and Charmides, one of the Ten, who was Plato's uncle (and Critias's ward). As for "acquaintances," Plato must have known nearly every one of them.

4. This man was Leon of Salamis, who had a distinguished political and military career under the democracy; cf. Nails (2002) sub nom.

and one least fitting Socrates: they prosecuted him for impiety,[5] and the people convicted and executed a man who had been unwilling to take part in the impious arrest of one of the friends of the exiles when it was their misfortune to be in exile. So when I thought about this and the kind of people who were involved in politics, and the laws and customs, the more I thought about it and the longer I lived, the harder it seemed to me to do anything right in politics. It is impossible to do anything without men who are your friends and trusted companions—these are not so easy to find ready-made, given the fact that our city no longer observes the customs and lifestyle of our fathers, and the possibility of acquiring new ones was not so easy, since the written and customary laws are corrupted and the evil increases with wonderful speed, so that, although I had once been so full of passion for public affairs, when I looked at all this and saw that everything was topsy-turvy, finally I became dizzy; I did not exactly give up thinking that at some moment these particular things and the regime as a whole might be better, but I was always waiting for the opportunity to act, and finally I understood that all existing cities have flawed regimes—the condition of their laws is nearly incurable without some amazing resources, and good luck as well—and so I was compelled to say, praising true philosophy, that from this alone we could look for justice in political affairs, and private affairs also. The peoples of mankind will never cease from evils until the race of true and proper philosophers arrive at political power, or the powerful persons in the cities through some divine dispensation really philosophize.

* * *

This was my thinking when I came to Italy and Sicily on my first trip. Once I got there that "happy life" as they call it there, bloated with Italian and Sicilian cooking, gave me no satisfaction at all—stuffing yourself twice a day and sleeping not one night alone, and all the other living arrangements that go along with this. There's no creature under

---

5. This is not quite right: Socrates was prosecuted on a charge of introducing "new gods which are not the gods of the city"—and also on a charge of corrupting the youth (Diogenes Laertius 2.40; see also Xenophon, *Memorabilia* 1.1.1).

heaven, cultivating these habits in his early life, who could ever become thoughtful—he's not going to be gifted with such a wonderful talent—nor could he ever be temperate, and it's the same story with virtue in general, nor could a city ever be peaceful with any kind of laws where the citizens think they have to spend extravagantly all they've got and suppose they should have no occupation except parties and drinking and elaborate sexual affairs. Cities like this can never rest from alternating tyrannies and oligarchies and democracies; as for a just and equitable regime, the powerful of these cities won't stand for one word about that. I had already thought these things out when I made my way to Syracuse—perhaps it was mere chance, but more likely some higher power was planning to set in motion the recent events involving Dion and Syracuse. There is a threat of more to come if you do not pay attention, as I once again advise you.

How do I mean my arrival in Syracuse was the origin of it all? When I came into close company with the young Dion and disclosed to him in our talk my sense of the best for man and counseled him to live in that way, chances are I was unaware that without knowing it, I was contriving somehow the future dissolution of the tyranny. Because Dion, ever a quick study and particularly so as to my discourses at that time, heard me with penetrating attention, beyond any young person I'd ever met, and was ready to live the rest of his life better than the rest of the Italians and Sicilians, embracing virtue rather than pleasure and luxury in general. So he lived a life rather irritating to those who stuck to tyrannical manners—until death overtook Dionysius [the elder]. After this, he realized that he was not alone in the way of thinking he had acquired by correct instruction; he observed and recognized it developing in others—not in many, but in some—and he thought that, if the gods would lend a hand, Dionysius [the younger] might be one of these and that if something like that happened the result for his own life and that of all Syracuse would be incredibly blessed. Furthermore he thought I needed to come without fail immediately to Syracuse to take part in this, remembering his own companionship with me, how readily it raised in him enthusiasm for the finest and best life; if he could now bring about his project for Dionysius, there was every prospect that, without slaughter and murder and the bad things that are now going on, he could establish a happy and true life for the whole country.

* * *

Dion thoroughly worked this out in his mind and persuaded Dionysius to send for me; he also wrote with his own plea that I come without fail immediately, before some other people got hold of Dionysius and diverted him into some life other than the best. He asked it this way (to tell it at some length): What better opportunity are we waiting for than that which by some divine chance is now before us? He then detailed the Sicilian and Italian Empire and his own authority within it, also Dionysius's youth and enthusiasm, how he was always talking about philosophy and education, how his own nephews and relatives were readily disposed to the message and life I always spoke of, and they were fully competent to bring Dionysius along, so that now, if ever, there was every prospect that it could actually happen: philosophers and rulers of great cities could be the same people.

These were his inducements and lots more of the same; my own view was rather fearful as to how it was going to work out with these young people—the enthusiasms of the young are rapid and often self-contradictory—but I did know Dion's character, that his soul was stable by nature and he was already middle-aged. So I thought about it and was of two minds whether I should respond and go—or what? Finally, I came down on the side of going. If ever I were to try to bring about my ideas as to laws and the regime, now would be the moment. I only had to succeed in persuading one person, and I would have brought about everything good.

* * *

It was with such reasoning and such audacity that I set out from home—not as certain people thought, but mostly ashamed of myself, lest I find myself to be literally empty talk, never willing to take hold of anything real and in danger first of all of betraying Dion's hospitality—and his people, who were really now at considerable risk—and then if something went wrong and he was thrown out by Dionysius and the rest of his enemies, and he came to me in exile and questioned me, saying: "Plato, I have come to you as an exile not for lack of infantry or cavalry to hold off my enemies, but of discourse and persuasion—just those means by which, as I well knew, you are able to turn young people toward goodness and justice and settle them in mutual friendship and alliance. You made no attempt to meet this need, and so I left Syracuse and here I am. But my condition is not the main reproach against you; rather philosophy, which you ever praise and say is disrespected by the rest of mankind, how is she not now betrayed along with me so far as you've had anything to do with it? If we were actually living in Megara, you would have come to help me when I called, or else you would have lost all self-respect. As it is, do you think you can cite the length of the journey and the extent of the sea voyage and thus escape being called a coward? Far from it." If he had said these things, how do you think I'd have had the face to answer them? So my arrival was rational and as just as anyone's could be—with the consequence that I left my own occupations—not such low matters, after all—summoned by a tyrant who hardly seemed fit for my discourse or for me. By so coming I cleared my account with the Zeus of Hospitality, and made myself irreproachable in the sight of philosophy, when it would have been disgraceful if I'd gone all weak and terrified and got my share of cowardly shame. And when I came—to make a long story short—I found Dionysius's whole environment full of faction and of slanders made to the tyrant against Dion. I supported Dion as far as I was able, which was but little, and after three months or so, Dionysius accused Dion of plotting against the tyranny, put him in a small boat, and sent him off in disgrace. After that all of us friends of Dion were afraid that Dionysius might accuse one of us of complicity in Dion's plot and punish that person. As for me, some kind of rumor went about in Syracuse that Dionysius was going to kill me, holding me responsible for everything that had happened. He, however, when he noticed that we were all in this state, was worried that our fear would have some serious consequence and took us all back into favor; to me in particular he spoke soothingly and encouraged me and asked me please to stay—because it wouldn't reflect any credit on him if I went, but rather if I stayed, which is why he made such a point of inviting me. We know that the invitations of tyrants come with an element of compulsion—and he took measures to prevent me from sailing away, moving me up on the acropolis and housing me where, so far from some ship captain taking me if Dionysius did not object, it could happen only if the tyrant himself sent instructions to someone giving orders to take me aboard; no merchant, not one of those in charge of departures from that country, would have let it pass if I set off on my own, any one of them would have arrested me and brought me back to Dionysius, especially given that the news going around was quite the opposite of before: Dionysus is wonderfully fond of Plato. Which meant what? The truth must be told. He grew continually fonder of me as time went on, as he got familiar with my disposition and character—in the sense that he wanted me to praise him rather than Dion and to be his special friend rather than Dion's, and he was wonderfully ambitious of that result. But as to how that would have happened, if it had happened, in the best way, he drew back from hearing that, from absorbing discourses of philosophy and getting close to me; he was afraid of what the slanderers told him, that he might get entangled and then Dion would have his own way. I stood it all, holding on to the first notion I'd come with, that he might somehow become passionate for the philosophical life. But he held out and beat me.

*   *   *

So the first time I visited Sicily to teach turned out just like that. Afterward, I went home and then came back when Dionysius, in all seriousness, sent for me. As to why I did *that* and how it went, that it was reasonable and just, once I have first given my advice as to what to do in the current situation, only then I'll go on to that explanation—and thus deal with the people who keep asking why I wanted to go the second time. This way some side issues won't get in the way of my main point. What I have to say is as follows:

Anyone who has advice to give a sick man leading an unhealthy life must first change that life, and if he is willing to accept that, go on to give him the rest of his recommendations. If he is unwilling, the one who gives up advising such a patient, I would consider medically sound, while the one who puts up with him is unmanly and unprofessional. It's the same with a city, whether one man rules or several; if the regime is set on the right course and then asks for detailed advice, a man of sense could advise such a one. Those who are quite astray from the right regime and are absolutely unwilling to go in search of it, making it a condition that the advisor leave the regime alone, don't touch it, it's death to touch it, but he's to give advice in service to their plans and passions, how *those* would be satisfied for all time most readily and immediately—anyone who'd endure this kind of advising I consider unmanly; a man would not endure it. This is ever my way of thinking when someone seeks my counsel concerning some critical issue in his life, for example concerning getting money or the care of his body or his soul; if I think him in some kind of shape in his daily life or that he will take my advice in the matter about which he consults me, I give my advice with a whole heart, rather than do something superficially appropriate and stop. If he doesn't ask for my advice in the first place, or asks for it but obviously isn't going to take it, I won't go to such a one on my own initiative to counsel him, and as for using force, not if it were my own son. If it's a slave, I would give advice, and if he refused it, I'd use force. But I don't think it pious to use force on one's father or mother—unless they're sick and out of their minds; if they're living a settled life which suits them—but not me—I'm not going to irritate them with useless criticism, nor will I flatter and truckle to them, seeking out gratifications of their desires, as if I could welcome a life I wouldn't live myself. So a sensible person should have the same way of thinking about his own city. If its regime seems to him a poor one, he should say so—unless speaking will be useless or get him killed—but he is not to use force to produce regime change; when the best city cannot be achieved without exile and murder, he should just keep quiet and pray for the best for himself and his city.

* * *

That's the way I would advise you, as I along with Dion thus advised Dionysius: first to live his daily life so as to be as much as possible in control of himself and to acquire trusted friends and allies, so that what happened to his father would not happen to him—his father took back many great cities sacked by the barbarians but was not able to establish in each a trusted regime of men who were his allies, not of various people from elsewhere nor even of his brothers whom he had himself brought up as they were younger, and whom he had raised from private lives to authority and from poverty to riches. Yet no one of these was he able to make a partner in his rule, although working with persuasion and teaching and benefactions and the claims of kinship. So he was seven times more ineffective than Darius. Darius did not have brothers to trust or people he had brought up, but only his partners in the subjection of the Mede and the Eunuch; he made a division of seven parts, each larger than the whole of Sicily, and found his partners trustworthy, not attacking him or each other, and so stands as an example of how a lawgiver and a good king should be—because he established laws that even now still preserve the Persian Empire. Even more, the Athenians, not refounding many Greek cities but taking them over still-inhabited (having survived barbarian attacks), all the same, held their empire for seventy years by maintaining friends in the various cities.[6] Dionysius, however, gathering all of Sicily into a single city and in his great wisdom trusting nobody, barely survived—because he was poor in trusted friends, and there is no better indication of virtue and vice than this: the absence or presence of such people. So Dion and I advised Dionysius, given his condition, which he inherited from his father—he had no experience of education or of the kind of companionship needed—so first . . .[7] then once he was set on the right path, he was to acquire new friends from among his relatives and of his own age, friends in harmony with him as to virtue. Most of all he should make friends with himself because he was wonderfully lacking in that—we didn't say this explicitly, it wasn't safe, but we hinted at it and armed ourselves with arguments about how men in general could make secure themselves and those who might follow them, while everything would turn out in the opposite way if he did not go in that direction. If he would proceed as we instructed him, if he repopulated the deserted cities of Sicily and bound them up with laws and regimes so that they would feel a kinship with him and with each other as to a common front against the barbarian, then he would not merely double his father's empire, but really make it many times larger. If all this happened it would provide

---

6. The fifth-century Athenians developed throughout their empire a network of so-called *proxenoi*, public guest friends or consuls, and *euergetai*, publicly acknowledged benefactors; these were recognized "friends of the Athenians."

7. Apparently at this point some words are missing from the manuscript tradition.

a basis for Carthaginian subservience greater than their subservience to Gelon—not as it is now, since his father was assessed to pay tribute to the barbarians.

That was what we said and urged on him, we who were conspiring against Dionysius, according to the stories being told on all sides; these stories, getting hold of Dionysius, sent Dion into exile and frightened the rest of us. To give you the short version of a long process: Dion came back from Athens and the Peloponnese and taught Dionysius a practical lesson. But once he had freed the people of Syracuse and had twice given the city back to them, they felt about Dion just as Dionysius had when Dion was trying to educate and raise him into a king worthy of empire, and on that basis to join him in a life-long partnership. Dionysius joined up with the slanderers who told him that everything Dion did was a plot to get the tyranny—with the idea that Dionysius, once intellectually seduced by education, would lose interest in the empire and turn it over to Dion, and once Dion had made it his own, he'd use some trick to expel Dionysius from the empire. These stories gained the victory in Syracuse then and also the second time they were told—a weird victory and a victory shameful to those responsible for it. As to how it happened, that is something you have to hear, you who are calling upon me to join your present enterprise. I came to the tyrant as an Athenian, Dion's comrade, his ally, intending to make peace instead of war—but in my battle with slander I was defeated. When however Dionysius was trying with honors and money to make me his friend and a witness in his defense as to the fitness of Dion's exile—in that he failed completely. Later on, once I had gone home, Dion recruited two brothers[8] in Athens; they hadn't become his friends through philosophy but through the regular kind of comradeship most friends have, which they create by entertaining each other and through taking part in the Mysteries. Now these two were to bring him back from exile, his comrades because of that kind of friendship and because of the resources they put into the expedition. But when they got to Sicily and observed that Dion was being slandered to the Sicilians he

---

8. One of these was Callippus, himself an Academic, who later arranged Dion's murder and took over the tyranny.

had liberated as someone who was plotting to become tyrant, they not only betrayed their comrade and guest-friend, but as good as killed him with their own hands, standing in arms as allies of the murderers. The shame and the impiety I for my part do not pass over—nor do I speak of it, because there are plenty of other people ready to descant upon that, and always will be—but what is said about the Athenians, that these men shamed the city, I object to that. I say that he who did not betray this same person was an Athenian, although he could have received money and plenty of honors as well—because he did not become his friend out of vulgar friendship, but through the alliance of liberal education, which is the only thing a sensible man will trust, rather than kinship of soul and body. So I don't think the killers of Dion should be a reproach to the city, as if they had been some kind of notable people there.

*   *   *

All this was said in the way of advice to Dion's friends and relatives. Furthermore, I have the same advice and the same things to say on this third occasion to you, my third audience: Sicily is not to be enslaved to human masters (nor is any other city, I would say) but to laws—because it is not good for the enslavers or the enslaved, for themselves or their grandchildren and posterity; the project is altogether toxic. Diminished and illiberal personalities are liable to snatch at such profits, men who know nothing of occasions for the good and the just, long-term or short-term, divine or human. I worked to convince Dion first of this, second, Dionysius, and now you as the third—so take conviction from me for the sake of third Zeus the savior, and then cast your regard on Dionysius and Dion: the one I could not convince now lives an ignoble life, while the one I did convince died nobly—in seeking the best for self and city. After that to suffer whatever comes is altogether fine and right. Not one of us is born immortal—nor if he were, would it make him happy as the many think—because no good or evil worth mentioning happens to anything soulless, but only to the soul while it is still with the body or when separated from it. We must ever really accept the ancient and sacred stories that inform us that the soul is immortal and comes before its judges and pays the greatest penalties when it is done with the body. This is what forces us to believe about the greatest wrongs and crimes that it is a lesser evil to suffer them than to commit them. The avaricious man, poor in soul, doesn't hear this, or if he does hear it, he can laugh at it (as he thinks); he shamelessly everywhere grabs whatever he wants, like a beast—he eats, he drinks, he goes for that slavish and graceless, miscalled divine, pleasure: sex—he stuffs himself with it, blind, unable to see the impieties mixed in with this grabbing, how bad for him are all the crimes which the criminal drags about with him as he strays about the earth—and when he returns beneath the earth he goes an altogether and in every way disgraced and miserable journey. That's what I told Dion—and more—and convinced him. So I am entitled to be enraged with his killers pretty much as with Dionysius because they did maximum damage to me and practically the whole human race, the killers because they did away with a man who wished to employ justice, Dionysius because he was never willing to employ justice anywhere in his government—where he had supreme power—and if philosophy and power had there been joined in the same man it would have been a light unto the nations—Greek and barbarian—and firmly settled this true doctrine, that neither city nor man will ever be happy unless life is lived intelligently with justice, either because they have found it for themselves, or because their character has been reared and educated by pious men justly. That was the damage Dionysius did. The rest is small stuff, the damage to me. And Dion's killer did not know that he was producing the same result. For I know with certainty, as much as it is humanly possible to be sure about people, that if Dion had taken over the government, he would have adopted no other system of government than this: for Syracuse first of all, his fatherland, once he had freed it from slavery and dressed it in the fresh garments of liberty, he would have used all means necessary to adorn⁹ the citizens with the best and most fitting laws, and then he would turn his energies to the next task, to repopulate Sicily and free it from the barbarian, expelling the latter and subduing the former more readily than Hieron did. If all this had been accomplished by someone just, brave, temperate, and philosophical, then that same view of virtue would have been generally

---

9. The word here translated means both "to bring political order" and "to adorn, like a woman."

accepted—just as, if I had convinced Dionysius, it would have come safely into being among practically all mankind. As it is, some deity or evil spirit produced an epidemic of lawlessness and godlessness and the last degree of stupid initiative, which plants and sprouts the worst of everything and finally bears for its creators the most bitter fruit— this for the second time[10] upset and ruined everything. So now, please, on this third occasion, let us use only words of good omen. I'll merely advise you—his friends—to imitate Dion, his love of country and his temperate way of living; try to carry through his policies with better fortune—what his policies were, I've already clearly explained; if there is one among you who cannot live the Doric life in the traditional manner but is drawn into that of Dion's murderers and the Sicilian life, such a person you should not recruit for any trusted or sound action; you should invite everyone else to the repopulation of all Sicily on the basis of equality before the law, and you're not to fear the Athenians. There are people there who are more virtuous than most men and who hate those bold guest-friend killers. If, however, this is a long-term program while the many and various conflicts between factions spring up and demand attention daily, each and every man who by divine good fortune has some small share of right opinion must know that the evils of faction will never cease until the victors stop holding grudges remembering the battles, for people exiled and murdered, so that they indulge in the punishment of their enemies; they must get control of themselves and make laws tending to please neither themselves nor the defeated party, and compel the latter to obey them with a double compulsion: by respect and by fear—fear because they show themselves stronger if it comes to force, and respect because they show themselves masters of their impulses, ready and able to submit to the laws. There is no other way for a city to rid itself of the evils of faction; otherwise factions and enmities and hatred and distrust are liable to continue indefinitely in cities in that condition.

Those who at any time take charge, if they want security, have to select through their own internal process those Greeks whom they

---

10. This refers to the joint expeditions of Heracleides and Dion, which resulted in the death of both. The first time, evidently, was Plato's failure with Dionysius.

discover to be the best—first of all elders, men with wives and children at home and with as many good ancestors as possible, famous men and all men of sufficient fortune—for a great city[11] fifty of these will be enough. These are to be sent for with an urgent request and adequate compensation, and once they have been sent for, they are to be requested to take an oath and instructed to make laws, giving a greater share neither to the victors nor to the defeated, but equal and common to the whole city. This makes the whole difference in lawmaking—because if the victors yield to the laws even more than the vanquished, everything is full of security and happiness and escape from all evils. Otherwise, do not try to recruit me or anyone else as a partner to people who do not consent to the instructions here written. These are akin to the policies that Dion tried, and I tried, to achieve in our care for Syracuse—in the second phase. In the first phase I tried through Dionysius himself to achieve the common good for all, but some kind of supernatural fortune brought it to naught. So now it is for you to try for a luckier achievement, with a fair destiny and some kind of divine luck.

* * *

Let this be my counsel and my letter as to my earlier visit to Dionysius. As to my later journey and voyage, that it happened both understandably and cautiously, what follows is for anyone who cares to hear it. I broke off my narrative of the first time I spent in Sicily in order to give advice to Dion's circle of family and comrades. To finish the story: I used whatever influence I had to get Dionysius to let me go. Conditional on peace—there was a war in Sicily at that time—the two of us reached an agreement. Dionysius said that he would send for Dion and me again once he had settled his empire so as to be more secure for himself; Dion should not think what had happened to him an exile but rather a shift of residence. I agreed to come on those terms. When there was peace, he did send for me; he asked Dion to wait a year, but I should just come. Dion at that point told me to

---

11. The Greek is literally "ten-thousand-man city"; the notional number of a major Greek city was 10,000 adult male citizens. Syracuse was actually much larger.

make the voyage and insisted. And in fact, a lot of reports came from Sicily that "Dionysius's passion for philosophy has amazingly revived now"—that was why Dion fervently insisted I should not refuse the invitation. I of course knew that this kind of thing often happens to young people in relation to philosophy; under the circumstances, I thought it safer to say a firm goodbye to Dion and Dionysius. I annoyed them both by answering that I was an old man and the way things were going, nothing would correspond with the agreement. After this, evidently, Archytas came to see Dionysius—before my own departure, I brought about guest-friendship and amity between Dionysius and Archytas and his Taras people and once I'd done that, sailed away—also there were others in Syracuse who had heard certain things from Dion and these people had passed them on to others, so they were full of philosophical misunderstandings.[12] I think they tried to converse with Dionysius on these topics as if he had absorbed the whole of my thinking. He generally has some gifts as to a capacity for learning, and he was wonderfully eager for praise. Therefore, he liked what people were saying and was ashamed that it should become obvious that he had absorbed nothing during my visit; that was the source of his wanting to get it straight. Furthermore, his love of praise weighed on him—as to why he didn't get it on my first visit, we went over that earlier in this account—so once I got safely home and refused his second invitation, his love of praise was threatened in case some people might think I despised his gifts and his character and that my disgust with his lifestyle made me unwilling to come. I must tell the truth and take the consequences, even if someone hearing of the event should think badly of my philosophy and conclude that the tyrant was right. The third time, he sent a trireme to make the journey easy, and he sent Archedemus, an associate of Archytas—thinking I took him most seriously of any in Sicily—and some other Sicilian notables. These all brought the same news: Dionysius had

---

12. "Philosophical misunderstandings": this phrase translates the rare Greek word *parakousmata*, which may have been coined for this passage. *Akousmata* is a Pythagorean term for the words of the Master as orally transmitted; here, Plato seems to be saying that certain things he had said were passed along but distorted and misunderstood.

15

made wonderful progress in philosophy. Also, he sent me a very long letter, knowing my relation with Dion and how Dion wanted me to sail and come to Syracuse. The letter was accordingly shaped so right from the beginning, starting like this: "Dionysius to Plato" and then after the usual formalities, the very first thing it said was: "If you will yield to us and come this time, in the first place the issues around Dion will be settled in whatever way you wish—I know your wishes are moderate, and I shall agree to them—but otherwise nothing will happen as you wish especially as to Dion's affairs." That was what he said; this is no time to go into the rest of it; it was long. Other letters kept coming from Archytas and the Taras people praising Dionysius's philosophy and saying that, if I did not come, the friendship I had created between them and Dionysius—which had substantial political implications—I would completely discredit. All this was going on in the time of that invitation, the people in Sicily and Italy tugging at me, those in Athens literally with their insistence as good as shoving me out, and it was still the same story: I must not betray Dion and my guest-friends and comrades in Taras. Also, I myself had a lingering sense that it was no wonder if a young person who had half heard some things worth knowing and who was talented should fall in love with the best life. So I had to put it to the test as to which way things were; I could not play the traitor here nor bring on myself such justified blame in case things really were as they were said to be. Therefore I went, veiled in rationalizations—full of fear and apprehending nothing particularly noble, you may be sure—but really I did what I did, dedicating this third time to Zeus the Savior. I was lucky to get back in one piece, and for this, I have to feel grateful to—after god—Dionysius; so many were plotting to kill me, and he held them off and showed some restraint in relation to me.

* * *

When I got there, I thought the first thing to do was to run a test: Had Dionysius really, as it were, caught fire from philosophy, or was all this talk that had come to Athens worthless? There is a certain way of making a test of these matters, not inconsiderable but really fit for tyrants, especially those stuffed with philosophical misunderstandings—as I noticed as soon as I arrived had exactly happened to Dionysius. You have to show people like this what kind of thing the whole of it is and what effort and labor it contains. Your listener, if he is really philosophical—suited to the thing and inspired to be worthy of it—thinks he has heard of a marvelous venture, that he has to join it, and there's no sort of life doing anything else. After that, he exerts himself and his leader in the venture, and does not let him go until he achieves the completion of it all, or gets the capacity to be able to find his way without the one who showed it to him. Such a man lives his life in this way and with these things in mind in whatever activity he may undertake; in everything he clings to philosophy and to the daily diet which most makes him quick to learn and gives him a good memory and able to think things out in sobriety; he continually hates the opposite sort of thing. Those who are not really philosophers but have a superficial sense of its content, like a skin-deep sunburn—these people, when they see how many things there are to study and how much work it is, and how moderation in daily life goes with this thing, they think it's too hard, something *they* just can't do and *they* couldn't live that way—but some of them still convince themselves that they've already pretty much heard the whole of it, and they don't need to take any further trouble. This experiment is clear and absolutely safe: it picks out those who pamper themselves and are unable to do the work and tells them not to blame the examiner but themselves if they cannot take on all the preconditions of the business. That, then, is what Dionysius was told. I didn't lay it out completely, nor did Dionysius ask me to. He pretended to know competently himself most of the main points from his other instructors. In fact I hear that he wrote something about my instruction as though it was his own work—not anything I told him; I know nothing of those things. I know there are some others who have written on these same things, but who in the world they are, they themselves don't even know. This is what I have to say to all those who have written and will write about what matters to me, whether they have heard it from me or from others or have discovered it themselves. In my view these people have no command of the thing.

 Nor is there now nor will there ever be any composition of my own about these things—because it cannot be put into words like other objects of study, but from long companionship concerned with the

Plato's Seventh Letter

d   thing and from living with it, suddenly as when a fire leaping across kindles a light, it comes to be in the soul and from that time maintains itself. And I know this, that if it were written or verbalized by me it would be done best—and when it's done badly, I'm as pained as anyone. If I thought it could be adequately written for the many and put into words, what would be a finer way for us to pass our lives than to write up such a great boon to mankind and bring its nature into the
e   light for all? But I think even the attempt to verbalize it is no good, except for some few who are able to find it themselves with minimal instruction; in the case of others, it fills some with an unearned sense of superiority, and others with a sublime and hollow hope, as if they'd
342   learned something really awesome.

                        *   *   *

      Now it comes into my head to say something more about these things—because maybe what I'm trying to say would be clearer once the following has been said. There is a certain true statement, oppositional to their rash attempt to write about these things anything whatever; I've said it many times, and I guess it needs to be said now. For each thing that is, there are three things through which knowledge of it comes to be,
b   and the fourth is that [knowledge]; then we have to posit a fifth, which is knowable and truly is—thus one is the name, second is the definition, third is the image, knowledge is fourth. If you want to know what this means, take one example and you'll have it all. There is something called a circle; its name is the word I just used. Second comes the definition, composed of names and phrases: what is equal in every direction from the edges to the middle, that is the definition of the name curved,
c   and round, and circle. The third is what is drawn and erased, turned on a lathe and perishable. None of these things, all of which are relative to the circle, happen to the circle itself since it is different from them. The fourth is knowledge and sound intuition and opinion concerning these things. All this we have to posit as single; it is not to be found in language nor in physical forms but is to be found in the soul, which
d   makes clear its difference both from the circle itself and from the nature of the three previously mentioned things. Of these, intuition comes nearest in similarity and kinship to the fifth, while the rest are further

off. The same holds for the straight together with the spherical shape, and for color, and for good and fine and just, and for every object, both those constructed and those existing by nature, for fire and water and all such things, for every animal and for every ethical quality of souls, and for each and every action and experience. For all these things, if you don't get hold of the four some way or other, you'll never participate in complete knowledge of the fifth. Furthermore those four try to show us the kind of thing each thing is, rather than its being, because of the weakness of language. That is why no one possessing intuition will risk putting into words his intuitions, especially into something not permitting revision, as is the case with published work.

Here's another way to understand what I'm saying. Any circle actually drawn or turned on a lathe is full of the opposite to the fifth circle—because it approximates to the straight at every point—while the circle itself, we say, has not the slightest bit of the opposite nature in it. Also we say no name of anything is stable; nothing prevents calling straight what we now call round and straight, round, and it will be no less stable for those who transpose and call oppositely [the names]; the same point applies to the definition, given that it is composed of words and phrases; it's never adequately stably stable. There can be endless talk about each of the four as to how unclear it is; the main point, as we were just saying, is that given two different realities, the being of things and the kind of things they are, while the soul endeavors to know what it is, and not what kind of thing it is, each of the four presents to the soul—in words and in concrete facts—what it is not looking for, ever providing to our sense an easily refuted description and representation in each case, and so they fill practically everybody with all kinds of bafflement and obscurity. So long as through comfortable idleness we have not acquired the habit of seeking the truth but are satisfied with whatever images present themselves, we shan't make each other ridiculous, answering questions we are asked, although the questioners are able to tear apart the four and refute us. But whenever we are compelled to answer with the fifth and clarify it, any capable person who wants to can win, and make most of the audience think—of anyone who expounds in words or in writing or in his answers—that he doesn't know what he's writing or talking about; they are unaware that sometimes the soul of the author or writer is not refuted, but rather

e

343

b

c

d

19

the nature of the four in each case, since they are fundamentally inadequate. But a long-term commitment to all this, traversing the upside and downside of each thing, can with labor bear knowledge when talent teaches talent. When talent is absent, as is the natural state of the soul of the many in relation to learning and to the habits of life we've been describing, that's a total loss, and not even Lynkeus[13] could make such persons see.

To sum up: if someone is not akin to the business, no skill of apprehension or memory will make him so—the starting point cannot be found in conditions alien to it—so that those who are not adapted or akin to what is fine in the case of justice or anything else, although in other matters they have apprehension and memory—nor those who are akin, but lack apprehension and memory—neither of these will ever learn the truth of virtue so far as it can be learned—nor of vice either. The falsehood and the truth of every reality must be learned together, with constant practice over a long period, as I said when I began. With difficulty in joint practice of these things in each case, names and definitions, appearances and perceptions, being refuted in friendly refutations, employing question and answer without ill will, then understanding shines forth in each case and intuition, focused to the furthest degree humanly possible. That is why no one who is serious about serious things will ever write and thus create a basis for human ill will and bafflement. From all this one can draw one conclusion: whenever you see someone producing written work, either the laws of a lawgiver or in any other form whatsoever, these are for him evidently something not particularly serious even though he himself is a serious person, while *those* things he laid away in the best part of himself—but if he really in all seriousness committed his thoughts to writing, "then, you know, they"—not gods, but mortals—"took away his wits."[14]

* * *

---

13. Lynkeus was one of the Argonauts and was said to be so sharp-sighted he could see through the earth.
14. This quotes the poet's comment on Glaucus giving gold armor in exchange for bronze (*Iliad* 7.360).

Anyone who has followed this story of my adventures will quite understand that if Dionysius or anyone small or great wrote something about nature's first and last things, he wasn't listening, nor did he get out of my discourses any sound understanding of what he wrote. If he had, he would have revered these things of mine and would not have dared to put them out so discordantly and unsuitably. Nor could he have written to keep them in memory—because there is no danger of anyone forgetting it, once he's got it in his soul; it's as brief as can be—but if at all, it was out of disgraceful vanity, either claiming personal authorship or claiming that he shared our education, of which he was unworthy in his very eagerness to be thought to have shared in it. If Dionysius got it all in one conversation, maybe so, but how that could be "God wot" as the Theban says—because I went through it, as I said, just once, and never after that. Then there is the next question to consider if you want to find out what happened and how it happened: Why was it that we didn't go through it a second and third time and many times? Was it because Dionysius, when he'd heard it once, thought he knew it and actually did know it, either by working it out himself or getting it somewhere from others, or because it is something trivial, or thirdly because he was not up to it, it was too much for him, and he really was not able to live devoting himself to good sense and virtue? As for triviality, plenty of witnesses will go into battle speaking on the other side, far more authoritative judges of the matter than Dionysius. If he worked it out or learned it, and it is a worthwhile part of the education of a liberal soul, then how, unless he's some kind of wonderful person, could he so light-heartedly have dishonored the leader and master of these things? As to how he dishonored me, I shall now relate.

* * *

Shortly after these events, whereas previously Dion had held on to his property and received the rents, now Dionysius stopped allowing the stewards to send them to the Peloponnese, evidently completely oblivious of his letter. They were to be not Dion's but Dion's son's, who was Dionysius's nephew and legally his ward. So matters had reached this point by then, and I had acquired a precise view of Dionysius's desire for philosophy, and I could complain (or not) all I wanted. It was already summer and the sailing season. Then I decided I should not be angry with Dionysius but with myself and with the people who'd made me come there for a third visit to the strait of Scylla "so that still I might take the measure of dire Charybdis,"[15] and I should say to Dionysius that it was impossible for me to stay when Dion was being so abused. He tried to soothe me and asked me to stay, not thinking he would look well if I went as a direct eyewitness of all this—but if I did not consent, he himself would arrange my passage. I was thinking of getting aboard some merchant vessel and sailing away, furious, ready to take whatever consequences if he stopped me, since obviously I wasn't doing anything wrong, but was being done wrong. But he, once he could see that I wouldn't agree to stay, devised the following device to keep me there that sailing season. He came to me the following day with this plausible speech:

"Let's get Dion and what is Dion's out of the way as a constant source of discord between us. I will do for Dion, with your help, as follows: I think it right that he should take his property and live in the Peloponnese, not as an exile, but as someone who can come here to visit when he and I and you, his friends, agree to it. This implies that he is not plotting against me; you and your people and Dion's people will stand surety for that, and he is to guarantee it. The property he takes, let it be placed in the Peloponnese and at Athens with whomever you all decide; let Dion have the revenue, but not have authority to withdraw it without you all—because I don't completely trust Dion to do right by me if he has the use of that money (it's a substantial sum); my trust is rather in you and your people. So see if you find that satisfactory, and stay for a year on that basis, and in the season depart taking the money with you. As for Dion, I am sure he'll be very grateful to you for making this deal on his behalf."

When I heard that speech, I didn't much like it, but all the same after thinking about it I said that on the following day I would send him news of my decision. That was the agreement for the moment. Once I was on my own, I thought about it, pretty upset. The beginning of my deliberation went like this:

---

15. *Odyssey* 12.428 refers to the final ordeal in Odysseus's narrative of his adventures.

"Well now, assuming Dionysius has no intention of doing what he says, if I go off and then he writes to Dion plausibly—he himself and getting others of his people to write—the proposition he has just made me, and says he was willing, but I was unwilling to do what he asked—I just blew off all Dion's affairs—and actually he won't be willing to send me away—he doesn't need to give direct instructions to any of the ship captains, he will find it easy to let them know that he doesn't want me to go—so then will any one of them be willing to take me as a passenger when I leave from Dionysius's house? (for along with all the other difficulties I was living in Dionysius's garden, and the doorkeeper was unwilling to let me out without written instructions from Dionysius) while if I stay a year, I can write to Dion as to my situation and how it goes with me. And if Dionysius does do some part of what he's said, the whole deal will be no laughing matter—for on an accurate valuation, Dion's property will not be less than one hundred talents—so, while it's true that if the project works out as is likely I'll have no idea what to do with myself, still maybe I have to endure another year and do a reality test of Dionysius's schemes."

That's what I decided, and the following day, I said to Dionysius: "I've decided to stay. I don't think it right, however, that you consider Dion my ward; I and you should send him documentation setting forth the present agreement and ask him whether it suits him or not, and if not, whether he wants something else and thinks it right, and that we should send this immediately, and in the meantime, you make no changes as to his property." That's what was said, that was what was agreed, as near as makes no difference. Then the ships sailed off, and it was no longer possible to sail and at that time, Dionysius raised with me a proposal that half of the property should go to Dion and the other half to his son. He said he was going to sell it, and once it was sold, he would give half to me to take away and keep half here for the boy. And that would be most fair. I was shocked by this declaration, and while I thought it was ridiculous to argue with him anymore, I did say that we should wait for Dion's letter and write back with this idea. He just went ahead and boldly sold the whole property, just as he wished and to whom, and never said a word to me about it, and so this way I, for my part, no longer talked to him at all about Dion's affairs. I didn't think it would be any use.

Plato's Seventh Letter

* * *

Up to this point, I had been trying to support philosophy and her friends. After this we lived together, I and Dionysius, I like a bird longing to fly off somewhere, he making shift some way or other to start me from cover—without parting with any of Dion's property. All the same, we claimed to be comrades in the face of all Sicily. Then Dionysius tried to lower the wages of his older mercenaries below his father's habitual level; the soldiers got angry and collected in a crowd and said they wouldn't stand for it. He tried to use force, locking the gates of the acropolis; they immediately mounted an attack on the walls, raising with a shout some barbaric warriors' hymn. Dionysus then was afraid and conceded everything, with an additional increase for the light-armed troops who joined in. Soon the word went around that Heracleides[16] had been the moving spirit of all this. As soon as he heard that, Heracleides hid himself away; Dionysius was looking for him without success when he sent for Theodotes to the garden—I was actually walking in the garden at that time—and while I don't know the rest of it nor did I overhear their conversation, I do know what Theodotes said to me in the presence of Dionysius, and I remember it: "Plato," he said, "I'm trying to persuade Dionysius here to agree that if I'm able to bring Heracleides here for discussion of the current complaints against him, and then it should be decided that he's not to live in Sicily, my understanding will be that he will take his son and his wife and sail off to the Peloponnese, and live there without damage to Dionysius, and receiving his rents. I have already sent for him, and I'll send for him again now, in case he will respond to my previous sending or to this one. My understanding and requirement of Dionysius is that if anyone finds Heracleides in the countryside or here, nothing bad will happen to him except that he will leave the territory and stay until Dionysius decides otherwise." "Do you," he said, speaking to Dionysius, "agree to that?" "I agree. Not even

---

16. Heracleides, evidently after Dion's exile, became the leader of the Syracusan opposition; when later Dion organized an expedition against Dionysius, Heracleides organized one with him. For a time, he and Dion cooperated, but eventually Dion found it impossible to control him, and had him murdered.

if," he said, "he turns up in your house, nothing bad will happen to him contrary to what you just said."

In the afternoon of the following day, Eurybios and Theodotes came in a rush to me amazingly upset, and Theodotes says: "Plato," he said, "were you not there yesterday when Dionysius gave his agreement in your and my presence concerning Heracleides?"

"Of course," I said.

"Now," he said, "light-armed troops are running around looking for Heracleides; he is probably somewhere or other. But," he said, "let us go to Dionysius without fail."

So we went and got where he was, and they stood by silently in tears, while I said: "These two are afraid that you might do some injury to Heracleides contrary to yesterday's agreement. I think he has returned and been seen somewhere or other." When he heard that, he flushed and turned all colors, evidently angry. Theodotes knelt before him, took his hand, and wept; he beseeched him to do no such thing. I then put in a word of encouragement: "Cheer up, Theodotes," I said, "Dionysius would never stand for doing something contrary to yesterday's agreement." Then he gave me a thoroughly tyrannical look and said: "I never made the slightest agreement with you." "Before the gods," I said, "you did, about the very things that they're now asking you not to do." With that remark, I turned and left.

After that he was hunting for Heracleides, and Theodotes sent messages to Heracleides telling him to run away. Dionysius sent Teisias and light-armed troops with orders to pursue him, but Heracleides, it is said, got into Carthaginian territory a few hours ahead of them.

After this Dionysius's long-standing plan not to give up Dion's property came to seem a plausible reason for enmity to me, and first he sent me away from the acropolis, with the excuse that in the garden where I was living, the women needed to perform a certain ten-day festival. He told me to stay with Archedemus for that time. During that time, Theodotes sent for me; he was full of complaints about what was then being done and found fault with Dionysius. Dionysius then, when he heard that I had gone to see Theodotes, made of this a further excuse for hostility to me, akin to the previous one; he sent someone to ask me if I had really gone there when Theodotes sent for me—and I said:

"Absolutely." "Well then," he said, "he instructs me to tell you that you do not do well preferring Dion and Dion's friends to him."

That's what he said, and he no longer sent for me to his residence, since evidently I was now the friend of Thedotes and Heracleides, and his enemy, and he didn't expect any goodwill from me, now that Dion's money was completely gone. So after that, I lived outside of the acropolis with the mercenary soldiers. I heard from various people, especially from some Athenian crewmen, my compatriots, that I had gotten a bad name among the light-armed troops and that some of them were threatening, if they could catch me, they'd kill me. So I figured out the following way to safety. I wrote to Archytas and my other friends in Taras, telling them the facts of my situation. They, finding an excuse of some kind of diplomatic business, sent a triakonter and Lamiskos, one of their people; when he arrived, he applied to Dionysius about me, telling him that I wanted to leave, and that he should please permit that. He agreed and sent me off with some expense money for the trip; as for Dion's money, I didn't ask for it anymore, nor did he part with any.

*   *   *

I found Dion in the Peloponnese at Olympia as a spectator at the festival, and I told him what had happened. He immediately called Zeus to witness and called upon me and my relatives and friends to get ready to punish Dionysius, charging him with guest-abuse of us—that's what he said, and he meant it—and in his own case with unjust expulsion and exile. When I heard that, I told him to recruit my friends, if he wanted; "As for me," I said, "you and other people practically forced me to share Dionysius's board and hearth and join him ritually; maybe he came to think—by many slanderous tongues—that I was conspiring with you against him and his tyranny, but even so he didn't kill me; he shrank from that. I'm hardly of an age to go to war with anybody, and I can be between the two of you if ever you have a mutual need for friendship and want to make something good happen. While you are bent on evil, ask someone else." I said this, hating my travels to Sicily and my failure there. Out of their distrust and inability to trust my mediation, they themselves brought on themselves all the trouble; none of that—as far as we can tell—would have happened if Dionysius had given Dion his money or complete compensation—because I could easily have kept Dion from the wish and the capacity—but as it is they went after each other and steeped everything in evil. And yet Dion's intention was just what I would say mine should be—or that of any moderate person—as to his own resources and friends and as to the city, namely he would intend by conferring all the benefits in his power thereby to reach the highest position in the highest offices. This is not to be done by enriching oneself and comrades and city through plots and pulling together conspiracies, out of poverty and lack of self-control, overcome by helplessness in the face of pleasure, going on to execute the property owners—calling them "enemies"—and then to hand out their wealth to one's collaborators and comrades, telling them that no one should say it's *their* fault if people find themselves poor. It's all the same if one becomes popular with his city through this kind of benefaction, passing decrees to redistribute to the many what belongs to the few, or takes charge of a great city, which controls many smaller ones, then redistributes to his own city what belongs to the smaller, with no kind of justice. Neither Dion nor anyone else would voluntarily enter upon such kind of power that curses the man himself and his posterity forever, but rather upon the most just and best regime and constitution, brought into being without the slightest amount of killing and death. So Dion acted in this case, preferring to suffer ungodly acts than to do them, yet taking care not to suffer them; nevertheless he stumbled on the brink of overcoming his enemies—and no wonder, because a godly man dealing with the ungodly, a temperate and sensible person, will not be altogether deceived about their souls, but perhaps it's no wonder if he has the experience of a good steersman who is not unaware of the coming storm, but does not recognize the mighty and unexpected magnitude of the storm and thus taken unawares is shipwrecked. That is exactly what happened to Dion. He was certainly not unaware of the vices of those who were trying to bring him down, but the level of their ignorance and malice and greed, of that he was unaware, and so they brought him down where he lies, and Sicily is condemned to infinite sorrows.

* * *

As for what counsel remains to be said, I have just about said it and let it suffice. As to why I undertook to return to Sicily, I thought that story should be told because what happened was so strange and irrational. If anyone finds that what has now been said makes more sense of it and thinks the reasoning that led to these events was adequate, then in adequacy and moderation, my account has been given.

COMMENTARY

Plato Despairs of Politics

Plato was born in 428 BCE, give or take a year, and into a Golden Age. The age of Pericles had just ended, Sophocles, Euripides, and Aristophanes were all producing, Herodotus and Thucydides were writing, the Parthenon was new, and Pheidias and Polycleitus were at work. This was a city that thought itself the center of the world: "The greatest and most famous city for wisdom and strength," as Plato's Socrates calls it (*Apology* 29d). Athens had built the first empire owned by any Greek city-state; if we take "all mankind" to signify "the Greeks and those immediately concerned with them," Thucydides's Pericles is accurate when he says (2.64.3):

> You know that you have the greatest name among all mankind for not giving way to misfortune, for having spent the greatest number of persons and quantity of struggle in war, and for your possession of the greatest power known up to this time; so that eternally for those to come, even if we go down at last (and all things are born to perish) the memory will remain that we were the Greeks who ruled the greatest number of Greeks, that we held out against the greatest number of enemies in alliance and individually, and that we inhabited a city best provided in all things and greatest.

Thucydides's Pericles sees Athens as an epic hero, mortal in act but immortal in memory; her exceptional greatness is glorious but perhaps (as in tragedy) holds the seed of its own destruction. Golden ages are uncomfortable; such bursts of local creativity are generally the reflex of ethical destabilization. When we hear Athens praised, it is well to remember that in the eyes of most Greeks, Athens was an outlaw state. The Spartans fought the Peloponnesian War for the same cause for which the Persian War was fought: the liberty of the cities; when the Spartans won, most Greeks must have felt reassured.

Plato was born early in that war; he was old enough to remember the disaster of the Sicilian expedition of 415–13 BCE and was a grown man by the final defeat of Athens at Aegispotomoi. When the news of this defeat reached Athens, Xenophon (*Hellenica* 2.2.3) tells us,

> a sound of wailing went up from the Peiraeus through the long walls to the city as each passed the news to another—so that night no one slept, not only mourning the dead, but even more themselves, thinking that they would suffer what they had done to Melos—a Spartan colony—and Histiaea and Scionae and Torone and Aegina and so many others of the Greeks.

These words remind us that the years in which Plato reached manhood were years of apprehension; the Athenians were facing the probability of a defeat that would bring with it the possibility of annihilation.

These were also the years of the radical democracy, the years after the death of Pericles, when, as Thucydides (2.65.10–11) says:

> Those who came after [Pericles] were more on a par with one another, and as each of them were aiming to become the first in command, they gave way in their policies to the pleasures of the people. From this resulted many errors, as one might expect in a great city with an empire, and particularly the expedition to Sicily, which was not so much an error of judgment regarding those to be attacked, as a failure by the people who sent out the army to recognize what was needed by those who had gone on the expedition. But concerned rather with their private quarrels concerning the leadership of the people, they made the military ineffective, and then for the first time reduced the politics of the city to mutual confusion.

For those not deeply invested in democratic institutions—and few high-status Athenians were—it was easy to think that those at the top played to the passions of the people and turned matters over to them. The errors that followed from this led to the conclusion that the cause of defeat was the democratic regime. In fact, the immediate result of the Sicilian disaster was a brief experiment (in 411) with an oligarchic constitution. The democracy was then restored, but after the final defeat, although Athens was not destroyed, the democracy was replaced by the odious tyranny of the Thirty, supported by a Spartan garrison—a regime remembered with infamy throughout the fourth century.

In the *Letter*, Plato begins his story by speaking of his experience of this regime (324b–326b): At that time, he assumed he would go into politics; the revolution against the democracy involved friends and relatives of his, and they asked him to join; they turned out to be a terrible regime, and even tried to compromise Socrates—and that was the beginning of Plato's doubts about a political career.

Then came the trial, conviction, and execution of Socrates. Plato remembered that Socrates had been convicted of impiety—in fact, this is a misremembrance: The charge was introducing new gods that were not the gods of the city, that is, not approved by an act of the Assembly. Plato's error reflects his incomprehension of the event. The trial of Socrates was an anomaly; mere disbelief was not a crime at Athens,[1] and the Athenians were notably tolerant of eccentricity. The execution of Socrates was another anomaly and a major trauma for all the Socratics. Like most anomalies, it happened as a confluence of multiple causes, a kind of perfect storm, bringing together Meletus's religious fanaticism; the distrust the Athenians felt for anyone who seemed abnormally pious; their memories of the atrocities of the Thirty and their knowledge that Socrates was linked to those people; Anytus's intention to warn the philosophers to stay out of politics; and Socrates's own moral rigidity, which required him to stay and stand trial, accept conviction, and be executed. This seems to have been one of those events in which nobody got what he wanted—except perhaps Socrates. Meletus did not succeed in making the trial about religion (Plato, *Apology* 36a–b is surely correct in saying that without the support of Anytus, Meletus would not have got one-fifth of the votes); Anytus was unlikely to have desired the execution of Socrates—he rather expected him to leave Athens, which is what the Socratics wanted him to do. Socrates's martyrdom was achieved in an atmosphere of muddle. The *Letter* calls it a chance event (325b).

Yet this event was apparently not in itself enough to disenchant Plato with politics; some years of meditation followed. Plato, after all, was born into the political class; if Athens was or could think herself the center of the world, Plato was born to be at the center of that center. Davies's great genealogical chart[2] shows Plato related by blood or by marriage to almost every

---

[1]. Disbelief only became impiety (*asebeia*) and thus subject to penalty when expressed publicly (though some public displays of disbelief were tolerated). A *graphē asebeias*, like all *graphai*, implied some wrong committed by the accused against the entire political community and thus could not be constituted by privately held beliefs about the gods. See Todd (1993), 310–11.

[2]. Davies (1971) Table I.

Athenian political figure and to many non-Athenians as well: to Solon the lawgiver and Peisistratus the tyrant, to the great Philaid clan: Hippocleides, Miltiades, Cimon, Thucydides son of Milesius (Pericles's last rival) and Thucydides the historian—and through them to the Corinthian tyrants Cypselus and Periander and to the Thracian dynast Olorus. Also, he was related to the competing Alcmaeonid clan: Megacles, Cleisthenes, and its adjunct members: Pericles and Alcibiades—and therefore to Cleisthenes the tyrant of Sicyon. He was also related to Alcibiades's rival Nicias; to the orator Andocides; and to Callias son of Hipponicus, "Who has spent more money on sophists than all others put together" (*Apology* 20a) and was in the fourth century both general and ambassador. The "relatives" Plato mentions as inviting him to join the postwar oligarchy included Plato's first cousin once-removed Critias, the leader of the Thirty, also Critias's cousin and ward Charmides, who was one of the Ten.[3]

Plato, in other words, was born to be part of the informal oligarchy that made democratic Athens work. He was one of the *gnōrimoi* (γνώριμοι), the "known people"; he was a *kalos kagathos* (καλὸς κἀγαθός), literally "fine and good"—a "gentleman." These are the men who, by some combination of property and family, were in a Greek city qualified to make themselves heard in debate and become visible in public action. Plato was not a rich man,[4] but he had property enough, and his family was of the best.

The term "informal oligarchy" deserves some explication. Athens, as we know, was a direct democracy; the people gathered in the Assembly were the sovereign. From a decision of the Assembly, there was no appeal—except an appeal back to the Assembly, to "the people, who are the law at Athens" (Pseudo-Xenophon *Constitution of the Athenians* 1.18), to reverse themselves. Any citizen, further, was entitled to address the Assembly; this was an explicit rule. The first question, then, is: How did they regulate debate? Debate opened with the question: "Who wants the floor?" How did the chair know whom to recognize? Once a month, the quorum of the Assembly was 6,000, and there must normally have been thousands present. It is obvious that all those with something to say could not have

---

3. The committee in charge of the Piraeus.
4. Davies (1971, 322) notes that the only liturgy on record for him was actually paid for by Dion.

spoken.[5] There is no evidence from the fifth century for any formal procedure; the alternative is something informal, a kind of backstage to the performance.

Unless Thucydides's *History* is completely fictional, major policy debates at Athens (and Syracuse) featured pairs of speakers on opposite sides. These speakers would normally have been drawn from the rather small pool—perhaps not more than a dozen—of men who usually addressed the Assembly, although there could be exceptions: Mytilene was defended by Diodotus, a man of whom we otherwise know nothing, but who was almost surely chosen by the Mytileneans for this task. How did he get on the program? Someone must have passed the word to the *epistatēs* (ἐπιστάτης) who presided.

Speakers had to be chosen from both sides; in this sense, the backstage was nonpartisan. It presumably consisted of certain senior members of the political class who knew each other and, to an extent, trusted each other. They had other tasks besides regulating debate—for instance, elections. These were by show of hands; since the numbers were too large to count, this approximates to election by acclamation: It is assumed that the winner's majority will be substantial. In fact, I know of only one person (in a fourth-century text, but set in the fifth century) who complains of losing an election: Nicomachides—and Socrates tells him that he deserved to lose (Xenophon, *Memorabilia* 3.4). It looks as though the Assembly was presented with a slate, and nominations from the floor had little chance. In any case, elections in Athens (except for the negative election known as ostracism) seem to have proceeded with a minimum of electioneering.[6]

---

5. In the one instance in the literature in which someone attempts to address the Assembly from the floor, the herald calls the police to silence him (Aristophanes, *Acharnians* 54); during the rest of the scene, the protagonist intervenes in debate with the kind of shouted comments that were evidently topical at assemblies; no one pays any attention to him except to tell him to "shut up and sit down" (59).

6. Three passages refer to fifth-century activity of clubs or societies on behalf of the election of their members: Thucydides 8.54.4; Plato, *Theaetetus* 173d; and Aristophanes, *Lysistrata* 577–578. All three of these could refer to activity in the backstage toward getting people slated. The election itself would then have been an anticlimax. Compare Aristophanes, *Acharnians* 598: Lamachos: "There elected me . . ." / Dikaiopolis: ". . . three cuckoos!"

Then there was the budget. Appropriations were made by decrees in the Assembly, completely ad hoc; who made sure that the numbers came out at the end of the year? In the fourth century, new officials were created to deal with this matter, but in the fifth century, this also seems to have been settled in the backstage. The new officials are a sign that in the fourth century informal budgetary processes were breaking down.

There are at least two events on the fifth-century historical record when the backstage seems to have failed. The first is the debate on Pylos (Thucydides 4.27–28). The Athenians are besieging a body of Spartan troops stationed on the island of Sphacteria in the bay of Pylos. The siege is not going well, and there is fear that with the coming of winter, they will have to abandon it. People blame Cleon for having induced them to refuse a previous Spartan offer; Cleon strikes back, saying that the news from Pylos is not true. The messengers respond by calling upon the Assembly, and if they don't believe them, to send inspectors to report; Cleon and a colleague are chosen inspectors. Cleon realizes that he will be forced to confirm the messengers and so goes on the attack, saying this is no time for inspectors; they should just send reinforcements. Furthermore, he mocks Nicias, a general, saying if the generals were but men, they would have taken the island and that if he were in command, he could do it. There is uproar in the Assembly against Cleon; Cleon, after all, is a demagogue, that is to say, a political figure with access to the Assembly, popular or at least populist, but not the sort of person Athenians would expect to hold office. Nicias mockingly says that if he thinks it's so easy, Cleon should take whatever forces he wants and try it. Cleon at first thinks this is mere rhetoric and agrees to go; when he realizes this is a serious offer, he backs off and says he's not the general. Nicias renews his offer, resigns his command, and calls the Athenians to witness. The more Cleon demurs, the more the Assembly yells at Nicias to resign and Cleon to take over. Cleon, supposedly unable to get free of what he's said, undertakes the command, saying he'll take only some light-armed troops and with them, will kill or capture the Spartans within twenty days (Thucydides 4.28.5).

> The Athenians were in fits of laughter at his boasting, while sensible people were gratified, thinking that one of two things would happen: either they would be rid of Cleon, which they rather expected, or if this failed, they would have defeated the Spartans.

At the end of the narrative Thucydides comments: "Cleon's promise, crazy as it was, was kept" (Thucydides 4.39.3).

Cleon asked for exactly the type of troops needed for the siege to succeed; it is plausible that he was cooperating with Demosthenes, the general in the field. His theatrical boasting and insults, his claiming, refusing, and then accepting command, were then an elaborate charade calculated to trick Nicias and the Athenians into giving him something he could never otherwise have obtained: the post of general—which he then continued to hold until he died in battle at Amphipolis. He had done something no demagogue ever did before him—or after him either: actually hold the office of general. The "sensible people," apparently including Thucydides, failed to see through the charade—failed to see that Cleon had found a way around them. The backstage had failed to exercise its authority.

My second example is the trial of the generals after the battle of Arginousai (Xenophon, *Hellenica* 1.7; Diodorus Siculus, *Bibliotheca historica* 13.101–103.2). Details of the two main accounts vary, but the general outlines are clear. In the battle—the last Athenian victory in the Peloponnesian War—twenty-five Athenian ships were disabled and left as wreckage in the open sea. A great storm blew up, and the wrecks were left to their fate; the survivors were not rescued, nor were the dead picked up for burial. The Athenians blamed the generals and deprived eight of them of their office; the generals in turn wrote letters blaming the ferocity of the storm and also a letter asserting that the task of rescue had been entrusted to Theramenes and other leading men among the trierarchs. Diodorus remarks that this letter was "the main cause of the trouble" since it earned the generals the powerful enmity of Theramenes.[7] In other words, the rest of the story results from a failure of the backstage: If the generals had worked with Theramenes to tell a common story blaming the storm, they would not have been vulnerable.

Two generals sensibly did not return to Athens; the other six were called to account before the Council, where it was decided to hold them for appearance before the Assembly. Xenophon describes this Assembly as an unruly occasion with a lot of shouting; Theramenes spoke against the

---

7. Andrewes (1974) provides reasons to think that Diodorus's treatment of the letter derives from the Oxyrhyncus historian.

generals, while the generals took the position that the storm was to blame—or that if anyone was to blame, it was Theramenes and his colleagues. This was good legalism—if you don't accept my first defense, then I ask you to accept the second—but it is rhetorically weak and no doubt left some people confused. However, the Assembly tended to support the generals, but as it was growing dark the matter was put over to another meeting, with instructions to the Council to bring before the Assembly a *probouleuma* (προβούλευμα), a draft decree.

In the Council, Callixenus drafted a proposal as follows: The Assembly was to act as a lawcourt, voting by pebble so that there could be an accurate count of individual votes; the generals were not to be allowed a defense on the grounds that the Assembly had already heard them in the previous meeting; all six were to be tried together and if convicted the penalty would be death and confiscation of property. The first of these proposals was evidently novel, the second dubious, and the third flatly illegal, violating an Athenian decree that required defendants in such cases to be tried separately. When Callixenus brought his proposal before the Assembly, he was immediately cited for proposing something illegal. "Some of the people supported this, but the majority shouted that it would be terrible if anyone should prevent the people from doing what they wanted" (Xenophon, *Hellenica* 1.7.12). Lysicles then proposed that those who had made the citation should be included in the same verdict as the generals; the people made a lot of noise, and the citation of illegality was withdrawn. Some of the *prutaneis* (πρυτάνεις), the presiding board, then said they would refuse to put the matter to a vote; Callixenus threatened them with inclusion in the verdict so that if the generals were convicted, the obstructive *prutaneis* would also die. The Assembly was turning into a lynch mob. All the *prutaneis* gave way—all except Socrates, who happened to be among the *prutaneis* on this occasion.

Clearly the Assembly was out of control. There is, however, a prior question: How did Callixenus induce the Council to accept his proposal in the first place? Prior action by the Council was supposed to ensure orderly procedure; in this case, it had the opposite effect. I can only suppose that Callixenus was one of those the Council was accustomed to trust and that he assured them his proposal had broad support in respectable quarters, with friends of Theramenes claiming to represent respectability.

At this point Euryptolemus, a cousin and ally of Alcibiades, somehow got the floor[8] and spoke against Callixenus's proposal, instead proposing that the generals be tried separately and allowed to defend themselves. These alternatives were put to a vote by show of hands, and Euryptolemus was successful. Some kind of procedural intervention—probably claiming that Euryptolemus had made an illegal motion in that he moved not simply to defeat a *probouleuma* but to replace it—caused the vote to be taken over again, and this time, Euryptolemus lost. (We are reminded again that the show of hands is a shaky procedure.) The generals were then convicted and executed.

No one came well out of this affair; it seems to have been another occasion in which nobody got what they wanted—except perhaps Socrates. Theramenes may have been the short-term winner, but his career was not advanced: when he was next elected general, he was rejected at his *dokimasia* (δοκιμασία), the courtroom inquiry into an elected candidate's suitability (Lysias, *Speeches* 13.10). (Once again, we notice that elections are not so important; the important outcomes are settled in court.) As for the people, Xenophon (*Hellenica* 1.7.35) says:

> Not much later the Athenians changed their minds and voted that those who had deceived the people should be indicted and provide bailsmen until they were tried, and that Callixenus be one of them. So he and four others were indicted and held under arrest by their bailsmen; later . . . they escaped, before trial. Callixenus came back when the men of the Piraeus[9] recovered the city; despised by all he died of hunger.

I would suggest that the breakdown of the proper backstage, the inner circle to which Plato by birth would certainly have been admitted, ultimately disenchanted him (*Letter* 325c–d).

> The longer I lived, the harder it seemed to me to do anything right in politics. It is impossible to do anything without men who are your friends and trusted companions—these are not so easy to find ready-made,

---

8. Nails (2002, 81) says that Socrates's objection gave Euryptolemus his opportunity; this is quite possible, but the text of Xenophon gives us only post hoc, not propter hoc.
9. See note 2 above.

given the fact that our city no longer observes the customs and lifestyle of our fathers.

The traditional political order was no longer working; the alternative that presented itself was "true philosophy." We shall see that true philosophy was to be, for Plato, the new and reliable source of friends and trusted allies.

Plato's First Voyage to Syracuse

Plato does not say in the *Letter* that the execution of Socrates was the definitive end of his hopes for a conventional political career; it seems that his disillusionment happened gradually thereafter. He did not leave Athens immediately, but after a few years, he went to Megara, where a circle of Socratics was collecting around Euclid, who was creating a philosophical school there.[10] These will have been formative years—Plato was in his thirties—and most probably the years in which he began to form his idea of "true philosophy." (He does not call Socrates his teacher, but his "older friend" and "most just"; this suggests that he did not find his philosophical vocation during Socrates's life, but rather in the company of the next generation [*Letter* 324e].) After a period in Megara, perhaps from there, perhaps after a return to Athens, he set out for the Greek West, for Italy and Sicily. He was forty years old.

Travel is normally mentioned in lives of the philosophers as an element of their education, but usually, it is travel to the Near East and Egypt, to the old civilizations. The West was quite the opposite: it was travel to the Greek New World, an open frontier. The oldest colonial foundations were at that time 350 years old, but new ones were steadily being founded, and on occasion, older foundations accepted new citizens. This area was exceptionally creative and well-stocked with poets and philosophers, historians, law-givers, architects, and city planners. Plato in the *Letter*, however, remembers only his shock at the debased hedonism of that society, given

---

10. Biographical material on Plato's travels in the following paragraph follows Diogenes Laertius 3.6.

over to food and sex; given their manner of life, he says, no city could "ever be peaceful with any kind of laws" (*Letter* 326c–d).

Certainly, Sicilian cooking was a byword all over Greece; on this, there is a large literature. We hear less about sex. The luxury of Acragas was rather evidenced in her massive temples and funeral monuments and in the lavish scale of entertainment and extravagant display at weddings and other occasions (Diodorus Siculus, *Bibliotheca historica* 13.82–84).

However, ostentation of every kind was certainly characteristic of ancient Sicily. It is also true that Sicilian society was seldom peaceable for any length of time. We might, however, prefer to see their lifestyle not as the cause but as a symptom of deeper issues.

M. I. Finley (1987, 20) asserts: "The Sicilian Greeks failed to make a success of the city-state." He is speaking, however, of Syracuse and the cities of the south coast: Selinus, Acragas, Gela, and Camarina. These were all Dorian foundations. The "Chalcidian" cities in the northern part of the island—Leontini, Catania, Messina, Himera—seem, as long as they did not suffer invasion, to have maintained relatively stable constitutional governments. Italian Locri, furthermore (culturally included in Sicily as the southernmost city on the Adriatic) was known in antiquity for being the only major Greek city other than Sparta to develop without the experience of tyranny.[11]

I believe that the critical difference lies in the conditions of landholding. The Dorian invaders found the exceptionally rich agricultural land of southern Sicily being worked by indigenous small-farmers; these they reduced to some kind of serfdom and thus created a Greek rentier class—called, at Syracuse at least, the *geōmoroi* (γεωμόροι), literally "those who share the land." These estates might be, by Greek standards at least, enormous; the actual farmers were serfs, in theory (and largely, in fact, historically) ethnically distinct.

The citizens of a Greek city-state ideally were small farmers who earned their modest livelihood in self-sufficiency and came together only on critical occasions—political and military. The army and the government were both composed of citizens who shared the status of adult free males; sovereignty was thus diffused; these smallholders were the ballast of political

---

11. For more on the particularity of Locri, see Redfield (2003).

stability. This status did not imply equality. Aristotle in fact remarks that some citizens must be wealthy; otherwise, the city will not have a tax base. In democratic Athens, the Assembly was sovereign; however, the rich were politically distinct—a man who paid the cost of a war ship in a given year, for example, also commanded it in battle. The rich men of Athens might own two or three farms as a reliable source of income; the remainder of their fortunes would be fungible, available for such projects as mining or loans to international traders. The Syracusan rich, by contrast, apparently received ground rents from considerable territories. The city-state was not engineered to accommodate this degree of inequality. The Locrians were the exception; even if they, like the Spartans, lived off rents from dependent labor, their stability, like that of Sparta, was secured by rigid political institutions aimed at limiting the effect of economic relationships.

In the absence of such institutions, the land-holding class, however well provided, was not secure; their very wealth was their weakness since it motivated others to attack them, usually a faction led by a prospective tyrant. The change of regime would be accompanied by the death or exile of some number of great landholders, and the distribution to a new set of their rights over their tenants. We are told (Diodorus Siculus, *Bibliotheca historica* 14.7.4–5) this happened early in the reign of Dionysius the Elder, in 391 BCE.

> He selected the best of the territory and presented it to his friends and to those who played subordinate roles under his leadership; he gave out the rest in equal shares to citizen and stranger, including in the name of citizen the freed slaves, whom he called "neocitizens." He also distributed houses to the mob, except for those on the Island—these he presented to his friends and mercenary troops.

Thus was established the community that Plato later encountered in Syracuse.

Such a community was inherently unstable since it came into being by sending powerful men into exile, men who (since Greeks could own property in more than one place) were not without resources and who were eager to use them to recover their position and to expel those who had expelled them. Sicilian tyranny, in other words, arose out of conflict within the wealthy class. Throughout the reign of Dionysius the Elder, we hear of Syracusan exiles based in the nearby cities of Catania and Messenia.

Dionysius's tyranny originated through his connection with Hermocrates, who appears in Thucydides as the leader of the "better sort" against the demagogues. During a period of constitutional government, Hermocrates led Syracusan resistance to the great Athenian expedition and commanded Syracusan ships against Athens in the Aegean during the last phase of the Peloponnesian War. In his absence he was sentenced to exile, out of fear he would become tyrant (Diodorus Siculus, *Bibliotheca historica* 13.75.5). Hermocrates died trying to force his way back in; Dionysius the Elder was severely wounded in this battle but succeeded in avoiding capture. After this event, he married Hermocrates's daughter and gave his own sister to Polyxenus, the brother of Hermocrates's wife: "This he did wishing to establish kinship with a distinguished family, and so secure the tyranny" (13.96.3). He then, once he could come out of hiding, called for the return of the exiles—namely, the faction of Hermocrates.

This civil conflict has a broader context. The character of all Sicily had recently fundamentally changed. The Carthaginians, who since 480 had been confined to a small area in the western corner of Sicily, had, by a series of campaigns in 406 to 404, succeeded in laying waste to the Dorian south-coast cities, gaining control of and largely depopulating them. Syracuse alone successfully resisted. In the course of this resistance, Dionysius, a man of modest origin,[12] came to be named *stratēgos autokratōr* (στρατηγὸς αὐτοκράτωρ), general with full powers. He held this office the rest of his life and used it to rule those parts of Sicily held by his mercenary armies. His reign, furthermore, was dominated by a series of unsuccessful wars that aimed to repeal the effects of the Carthaginian conquest and expel them from Sicily altogether.

This military authority Dionysius developed into an unusual type of tyranny. He turned the acropolis of Syracuse—actually not a high point, but a low-lying off-shore island, Ortygia, containing the two main temples, to Apollo and Athena, and connected to the mainland by a causeway—into his private fortress, fortified against the town and sheltering the fleet in

---

12. He seems to have begun as a secretary (Diodorus Siculus, *Bibliotheca historica* 13.96.4) or even a *hypogrammateus* (ὑπογραμματεύς), an undersecretary to the military command and was mocked in later life for beginning his military career thus. Cf. Diodorus Siculus, *Bibliotheca historica* 14.66.5.

its harbors. Here, he lived with his personal followers and private army. The town on the mainland—the largest city in Sicily and second only to Athens in all of Greece—was left formally independent; its council continued to meet, make laws, sign treaties, and so on. Of course, since Dionysius had his mercenary army, the town would respect his wishes. Furthermore, the remainder of Sicily was treated as a militarized area under the authority of the Syracusan commander in chief. Dionysius is styled in treaties *archōn Sikelias* (ἄρχων Σικελίας), ruler of Sicily—but not ruler of Syracuse.

Probably, Plato did not meet Dionysius the Elder—the *Letter* makes no mention of a meeting, and in 389/388, Dionysius was deeply engaged in the siege of Rhegium (Caven 1990, 169). The anecdotes in later sources of their conversations most likely were invented in the literary tradition of meetings between Wisdom and Power—a tradition that goes back at least to Herodotus's chronologically implausible meeting between Solon and Croesus and was renewed in Xenophon's historical fiction concerning a conversation between Simonides and Hieron.

Plato surely did, however, meet Philistus, who seems to have been in charge during Dionysius's absence ("Captain of the Citadel"—Caven, quoting Plutarch, *Dion* 11). He will be an important character in our story. He comes on the scene as Dionysius's patron immediately after Hermocrates's death (Diodorus Siculus, *Bibliotheca historica* 13.91.3–4):

> No one ventured to state an opinion concerning the war, but when they were all baffled, Dionysius . . . accused the generals of betraying matters to the Carthaginians and worked up the populace to punish them, calling on them not to be held back by babble about lawfulness, but to take justice into their own hands. When the magistrates fined Dionysius according to the law concerning incitement to riot, Philistus—the one who later wrote the *History*—as he was very wealthy, paid the fine and told Dionysius to say whatever he wanted—and he further said that if they wanted to impose fines all the day long, he would pay them.

From this point onward—for some forty years—Philistus remained loyal to Dionysius the Elder and to Dionysius the Younger after him. His "Thucydidean" histories (which are lost) presumably displayed his objectivity and realism. He was already rich and, in this sense, did not need the tyrant's favors. He quite probably supported the tyrants through a not-irrational and even perhaps reasonable conviction that, in the circumstances, military autocracy was the best government Syracuse could expect to achieve—mirroring Thucydides's opinion that the Athenians' fear of Alcibiades's tyrannical ambitions lost them their chance to win the Peloponnesian War.

If (as seems likely) Philistus was in charge of Dionysius's garrison and Ortygia during Plato's first visit, it would have been Philistus who sent Plato home on a Spartan ship. This was not a friendly act and is the probable source of the story that Dionysius the Elder sold Plato into slavery, so an Athenian friend had to buy him out. Apparently, what happened was this: The ship did not take him to Athens but to Aegina, the off-shore island closest to Athens. Aegina was at war with Athens at that time, and Plato was held as an enemy alien.[13] Greeks regularly held prisoners in a kind of fiction of slavery; there was no prospect that Plato would be put to heavy labor, but his captors could extort a ransom. This treatment of prisoners is already in the *Iliad*.

In the *Letter*, Plato does not mention Philistus; he mentions only one person he met in the West, namely Dion. In Plato's narrative that encounter was the critical, the only meaningful, event of the journey. "Dion," he says, "ever a quick study and particularly so as to my discourses at that time, heard me with penetrating attention, beyond any young person I'd ever met" (*Letter* 327a–b). Dion was then about twenty years old; Plato had just turned forty, and while he had begun to write and publish, was probably not yet famous. His "true philosophy" was still in the course of development and had not yet found the audience that later formed in the Academy. To encounter a rich and talented young person whose attention certified his philosophy's value would have been, for Plato, a life-changing experience. The intensity with which Plato, in the *Letter*, describes Dion's qualities suggests that the older man fell in love with Dion—and it may be that this was required. In any case we know of no other relationship in Plato's life that could plausibly be a source of his account of philosophical Eros in the *Phaedrus*.

Aristotle (*Politics* 1306a) says that Dion's father Hipparinus had installed Dionysius as tyrant; there is a tradition, which may have been concocted later for political reasons, that Hipparinus originally held the office of *stratēgos autokratōr* jointly with Dionysius. In any case, Hipparinus played

---

13. Caven (1990), 147.

a part. Aristotle takes him as an example of an oligarch who makes a revolution because he has wasted his property by extravagant living. This tells us that Dion's father belonged to the land-holding class; yet, if we are to believe Aristotle, Hipparinus's extravagance could well have been a lesson in moderation to his son.

Whether through his father or Dionysius, Dion was, in any case, extremely rich. Plato estimates his property to be something over one hundred talents[14] (*Letter* 347b). There is some ambiguity as to the use Dion made of his wealth. Plato is absolutely clear that the foundation of philosophy is moderation (see especially *Letter* 340b–341a), and he explicitly says that Dion, after meeting Plato, "lived a life rather irritating to those who stuck to tyrannical manners" (*Letter* 327b). Plutarch, however, does not mention moderate life as the cause of irritation but gives a rather different account (Plutarch, *Dion* 8):

> It was to be expected that Dion was irritating since he took no part in youthful enjoyment—and that is why they slandered him by giving plausible pejorative names to his virtues. His dignified reserve (*semnotēs*) they called contempt and his frank speech (*parrēsia*) arrogance (*authadeia*). When he sought to correct them (*nouthetein*), he seemed prosecutorial, and when he would not join their vices, he seemed to despise them personally. Actually, his character was naturally rather heavy and harsh, unapproachable in conversation and hard to deal with. Not only for a young man whose ears had been stuffed with flattery was he an uncomfortable and difficult companion; many also of those most involved with him, while they admired his straightforward, fine character, found fault with his manners, which were more rude and rough than is politically suited to those who required dealings with him. Even Plato later wrote to him—prophetically, as it were—that he should restrain his arrogance, suited only to a solitary life.

These are not marks of an unphilosophical nature: both *semnotēs* and *authadeia* were attributed to Socrates. Dion, however, had no share of

---

14. A talent functions as a unit of capital; the income returned by one talent was, in ancient Greece, enough to constitute a minimum livelihood. In modern terms, Dion's wealth should have provided him with an income about one hundred times the poverty level.

Socratic poverty. "He owned a great estate," says Plutarch, "and reached nearly a tyrannical level in display and possessions" (*Dion* 15). When Dionysius the Younger sent Dion into exile, he sent two boatloads of possessions after him, and, so long as the tyrant transmitted to him his rents, Dion lived large in old-world Greece.

Dion's conversion to philosophy, in other words, by no means prevented him from living the life of a Sicilian grandee. He was indeed fitted by birth, wealth, and talent to cut an important figure in the court politics of Syracuse. Evidently, he became one of Dionysius the Elder's most important agents; however, we have no details, only Plutarch's assertion that he was able to speak to the tyrant with *parrhēsia*, which is to say "frankness, absence of deference" and that he was nevertheless valued and trusted by Dionysius, and "carried through his most important embassies, being sent to Carthage" (*Dion* 5). Dion kept up his Carthaginian connections throughout his life.

We remember that Plutarch tells us that Dionysius had married into Hermocrates's family in order to secure his tyranny. After the death of his first wife, he married, presumably out of a similar motive, Aristomache, daughter of Hipparinus—and Dion's sister. Through this woman, the elder Hipparinus had two grandsons, both named Hipparinus. One was the son of Dionysius by Aristomache, and therefore Hipparinus's grandson through his daughter. The other was the son of Arete, daughter of Aristomache; his father was Dion—Dion married Arete, his sister's daughter and, therefore, his niece. This Hipparinus was the elder Hipparinus's grandson through his son—and also his great-grandson through his granddaughter Arete. It follows that Dion was both Dionysius the Elder's brother-in-law and his son-in-law.

This tangled web of affinity was made even more problematic by Dionysius the Elder's unique marriage arrangements. He married Aristomache (in 397) on the same day he married Doris of Locri; it was a well-kept secret which marriage was consummated first, and thereafter he slept with them on alternate nights (*Dion* 3). The marriage with Doris seems apt for securing Dionysius's alliance with Locri, a city that became of great importance to Syracuse. Dionysius the Elder spent his whole career, as already noted, on an unsuccessful attempt to drive the Carthaginians from Sicily; the resources for this enterprise were, however, collected by expanding his empire in Italy. Locri, the southernmost Italian city on the Adriatic side, became his base as he worked his way northward up the Adriatic. The union of Italy and Sicily, thus, was inscribed by Dionysius on his marriage bed.

This does not, however, wholly explain the marriage arrangements. These seem intended to prevent either wife from having the status of secondary wife or concubine; both were primary. This defined and limited Dion's relation to Dionysius's family. The two were related by exactly half a wife—or less, after Doris produced the first son, the heir, Dionysius the Younger. A story about Dionysius's last days may well be gossip, but it does represent the problem (Plutarch *Dion* 6):

> Once Dionysius's disease was thought to be fatal, Dion sought to speak with him about Aristomache's children; however, the doctors, favoring the heir apparent, would not give him the opportunity. Timaeus further says that they gave Dionysius a sleeping drug making him unconscious, with death following that sleep.

Dion, however, continued to be energetic. Plutarch continues (this may also be from Timaeus):

> For all that, when the first gathering of the young Dionysius with his friends took place, Dion spoke so opportunely about their interests that all the others seemed mere children in their thinking, and as to their frankness, mere slaves of the tyrant, since mostly ignobly and fearfully they gave such counsel as would please the boy—they were mostly paralyzed by their fear of the danger of Carthage hanging over the city. He, for his part, proposed, if Dionysius wanted peace, to sail straight to Libya and settle the war on the best terms: If, however, he wanted war, he would support it with his own funds and provide for his war fifty triremes fully launched.

Thus, as we shall see, the political stage was set for Plato's second voyage to Syracuse.

Philosophical Politics

In the West, philosophy was engaged with politics from its very beginning. Parmenides wrote the laws of Velia, apparently with such success that this city received a special dispensation from the Romans to retain the use of the Greek language.[15] Empedocles was offered a kingly crown, which he refused, but he was known to be the teacher of Gorgias, who carried a refined art of political rhetoric to old-world Greece.[16] The philosopher most significantly engaged with politics, however, was Pythagoras.

Pythagoras was born on Samos and resided there for the first half of his life.[17] We are told that he was a student of Pherecydes of Syros, who wrote a prose theogony describing the universe as the result of a marriage between *Zas* (Form) and *Chthonie* (Matter); the material universe was a wedding gift from *Zas* to *Chthonie*, a robe on which was embroidered the entire cosmos.[18] This text is dated in the mid-sixth century BCE, making Pherecydes the earliest identifiable proponent of the novel religious tendency we call "Orphic"; he also is said to have introduced into Greece the doctrine of metempsychosis, for which Pythagoras was later famous.

Pythagoras was an Orphic.[19] Ion of Chios, a good fifth-century source, tells us that Pythagoras wrote poems under the name of Orpheus (frag. 2 in *Die Fragmente der Vorsokratiker*). In middle life, Pythagoras emigrated to the Greek West—to Croton—where he found new opportunities. He gained disciples there and evidently formed around himself something like

---

15. For Parmenides as law-maker, see Diogenes Laertius 9.23.
16. Diogenes Laertius, 8.58, 63.
17. Biographical material on Pythagoras in this and the following paragraph follows Diogenes Laertius 8.1–3.
18. Diogenes Laertius, 1.119.
19. I use this term not to suggest that Orphism was an organized religion; it was rather a tendency, like that of New Age. The Greeks applied the label to a great variety of enterprises; some required a vegetarian diet, many included ecstatic states, for which the Greek name is "Bacchic"; there were Orphic writings—the ritual sometimes included a child reading from a book; there were specific burial practices and novel creation myths. The one thing all the Orphics seem to have had in common was a belief in personal immortality, including an idea that certain practices, especially ritual practices, can secure a better afterlife. (In these terms, Pherecydes was nearly an Orphic; we don't hear anything about his rituals, however.) Greek literature up to this time did not represent rituals intended to affect the afterlife; the epics told a variety of stories, but generally, the most that could be expected was a kind of minimal insubstantial existence in the company of powerless ghosts. That is the standard Homeric doctrine. Orphism thus sharply broke with Greek traditional religion and education.

a cult. There were secrets (Aristotle reveals one of them—there are three kinds of rational beings: men, gods, and Pythagoras).[20] There were prohibitions: "Do not stir the fire with a knife"; "Do not take swallows into the house"; "Do not eat beans." There were questions and answers: "What are the islands of the blessed? The sun and the moon"; "What are the Pleiades? The lyre of the Muses" (Riedwig 2005, 73f). These were called *sumbola*, which in ancient Greek means "a token of connection between two persons." Perhaps they functioned like a secret handshake.

The Pythagoreans were ideologically united in special bonds of friendship—in fact, their name for themselves was *hoi philoi*, the Friends. Someone called them *philosophoi*, perhaps originally in ridicule (as the modern Friends were called Quakers by their enemies but soon adopted the name as their own). In any case, we are told that Pythagoras was the first to be called *philosophos*.[21]

There is an anecdote concerning Pythagorean friendship that has the look of a folk tale; Aristoxenus (frag. 31 [Wehrli]), however, testified that it was told to him by Dionysius the Younger as an autobiographical fact:

> Aristoxenus tells us . . . that when Dionysius had lost the tyranny and had come to Corinth "he many times told us about Phintias and Damon the Pythagoreans. He said that there were some of his companions who were always bringing up the Pythagoreans, disparaging and mocking them and calling them fraudulent, saying that their high-and-mighty ways, their pretended Faith and Truth would be knocked out of them if they were subject to any real threat. Others denied this and as there was a dispute about it they set up the following scene for Phintias:
>
> "Dionysius sent for Phintias and confronted him with an accuser, saying that he had been caught conspiring against him, and that there were witnesses, and that the complaint against him was completely plausible. Phintias was dumbfounded by this information, but Dionysius just stated flatly that he had made a thorough investigation and that Phintias must die. Phintias then said that given this decision he thought it proper to ask for the rest of the day to settle his affairs and those of Damon. The two men lived together and shared everything, but as Phintias was the

---

20. Aristotle *Fragmenta selecta*, 132.
21. Diogenes Laertius 1.12.

elder he had taken over most of the household management. His request was that he be let loose for this purpose leaving Damon in his place.

"Dionysius said he was amazed and asked if there existed anywhere a person ready to stand substitute for another on a capital charge; Phintias said there was, and so Damon was sent for, and once the whole thing had been explained to him he said he would stand substitute and stay until Phintias should come. Dionysius said he himself was immediately impressed by all this; those who had originally organized the experiment however made fun of Damon saying he was going to find himself trapped, that he was the deer substituted for human sacrifices—but just as the sun was already setting Phintias arrived ready to die, upon which all were impressed and quite swept away. Dionysius said that he for his part then embraced and kissed the two men and asked that he himself might be enrolled as a third party to their friendship; they replied that however he persisted they would never stoop so low." Aristoxenus said he had this story from Dionysius himself.

The sting of the anecdote clearly is in the tail: Pythagorean friendship was a special bond, not to be shared with an outsider—and no one was more of an outsider than a tyrant. The story also tells us something about the presence of philosophers at Syracuse, and for that matter, something about Dionysius the Younger's rueful self-presentation at Corinth, where he took up residence in his final exile and became a kind of tourist attraction as an ex-tyrant. The present relevance of this anecdote, however, is to the emphasis in the *Letter* (331d–332d) on the political value of friendship:

> I along with Dion thus advised Dionysius: first to live his daily life so as to be as much as possible in control of himself and to acquire trusted friends and allies, so that what happened to his father would not happen to him . . . Dionysius [the Elder] . . . in his great wisdom trusting nobody, barely survived—because he was poor in trusted friends, and there is no better indication of virtue and vice . . . So Dion and I advised Dionysius . . . to acquire new friends from among his relatives and of his own age, friends in harmony with him as to virtue.

Although the Pythagoreans originated in Italy, they were already in Plato's time a presence in his world. Sometime in the 420s, when Plato was still a child, a wave of Pythagorean refugees arrived in old-world Greece; they gathered in various cities, most notably in Thebes and Phlius in Arcadia. Aristoxenus knew these as "the last of the Pythagoreans" and our knowledge of early Pythagoreans in Italy is primarily based on what they had to tell him. Their stories were various but had an overall political theme. It seems that Pythagoras and his followers had taken control of Croton and various other cities in Italy, only to provoke a reaction that resulted in riots and their expulsion from the West. Refugee accounts are seldom reliable; furthermore, their narratives, in so far as they included Pythagoras himself in the whole drama—of initial success and ultimate failure—were chronologically impossibly compressed. Not one of them can have known the Master personally, except possibly for a few as children. Nevertheless, their refugee condition was itself evidence that they had provoked political resistance.

Interestingly, these last Pythagoreans—who received enough public notice to make fairly frequent appearances in fourth-century Middle Comedy—made no known attempt at political action in old-world Greece. Nevertheless, they presented a model for philosophical politics. By their own account, their superior purity and virtue qualified them for power, and their solidarity in friendship provided the means to obtain it. More than one modern author has compared them with the eighteenth- and nineteenth-century Freemasons. A disciplined group that maintains secrecy can be perceived, not unrealistically, as a conspiracy. One of our sources tells us that for a time, 300 Pythagoreans in Croton belonged to the governing body of 1,000, and this number was able, without declaring themselves, to determine all public matters.[22] The Pythagorean narrative, in one of its versions, thus provided a model for the informal oligarchy which, according to Thucydides (8.66.1), actually came into existence at Athens in 411 BCE:

> The Assembly and the council drawn by the lot continued to meet, but they made no decisions which had not been decided by the conspirators; also, those who took the floor were drawn from this group, and their speeches had been reviewed ahead of time by them.

There is every reason to believe that the arrival of the Pythagorean exiles had a considerable effect on the Athenians, especially on Socrates.

---

22. Diogenes Laertius 8.3

These Pythagoreans would have been the first self-identified philosophers Plato met.[23]

Plato implies in the *Letter* (326b–c) that his views concerning the decadence of the Greek West were firmly established by the time he arrived in Syracuse; however, he speaks only vaguely of "Italian and Sicilian cooking." He most probably visited Taras, modern Taranto, on his way to Syracuse; this is the first Greek city one would reach upon crossing the Adriatic. Taras was the last Italian city hospitable to Pythagoreans. There is only one reference to this city in Plato's works outside of the letters—so vivid that it suggests personal experience. The Spartan in the *Laws* (637b–c) remarks: "In Taras I beheld the whole city drunk for the Dionysia." The Athenian replies: "There is one answer that resolves the issue. . . . Anyone will answer the stranger who is shocked when he sees something he's not used to: 'Do not be puzzled, stranger. This is our custom (*nomos*); you may have a different one in this very situation.'" We can imagine Plato as just such a puzzled stranger. It would seem that Taras, in his time, was not particularly ascetic and, in this sense, at least not dominated by Pythagoreanism.

Diogenes Laertius (3.6, citing no source; perhaps he merely thinks "Plato must have sought those people out") says that Plato traveled to Italy to the Pythagoreans Philolaus and Eurytus. These were older than Plato. Philolaus's meeting with Plato may be legendary—it is not even certain that he was still living at the time of Plato's first visit to the West. But if they did meet, it was probably in Taras. There, Plato might also have met Archytas, who was roughly his own contemporary. Archytas is said to have been a pupil of Philolaos and Eurytus—that is, they stood to Archytas as Socrates stood to Plato. Archytas—and therefore Taras—will become important in our story later.[24]

Philolaos, Archytas's teacher, was a second-generation Pythagorean; he was among the first who wrote and published texts, in contrast to the Master, who, according to tradition, like Socrates, published nothing. In the second generation, the Pythagoreans split, between the conservatives

---

23. Since words of the *philosoph-* root occur nowhere in Aristophanes's *Clouds*, it is probable that the historical Socrates did not call his activity *philosophia*, at least by 423; however, he may have adopted the term by the time Plato knew him.

24. See Huffman (2005), 7.

(so-called "Acousmatics"), who maintained an oral tradition claiming to transmit the authentic teachings of the Master, and the Mathematics, who wrote and published on scientific topics, mainly mathematics and harmonics, and also on politics.

Archytas was a third-generation Pythagorean and a Mathematic. He was a philosopher and a scientist; he is said to have founded a mechanics based on mathematical principles; he also wrote on music (Diogenes Laertius 8.83). Furthermore, he was a political figure; we are told (Diogenes Laertius 8.79) that "he seven times held the public *stratēgeia* [evidently the leading office in Taras] although no one else had held it more than once, since the law forbade that." We should like to know just which years those were, but it seems probable that they coincided with Plato's second and third visits to Syracuse since it is clear that Archytas was the leading figure in Taras at that time.

Alphonso Mele (2002, 80) has suggested that Taras up to the mid-fifth century, was preoccupied with protecting and perhaps expanding its frontier to the north with the Iapygians—Indo-European speakers who occupied the Salentine peninsula (the heel of the "boot")—but that in the late fifth century, Taras turned her attention toward southern Italy, a change signaled by her foundation of Heracleia in 433/432.

Archytas evidently inherited this concern with Taras's southern frontier, a concern made acute by the threat of the Lucanians, an Italic people who were moving south through Italy and who sometime in the fifth century, got far enough to take over Paestum, on the Tyrrhenian side. Archytas in the fourth century became *stratēgos* of the Italian League, which joined Taras militarily with the Adriatic cities Metapontum and Heracleia in resistance to the Lucanians. This was the League that replaced the earlier version farther south, based on Thurii; that League had been crippled by Dionysius the Elder. The reconstructed League may well have been Archytas's work.

Taras shared with Syracuse a common interest in preventing the Lucanians from penetrating the Adriatic coastal plain; on the other hand, as Syracuse moved northward and Taras reached toward the south, the two cities seemed destined to be enemies. This ambiguous relation, I shall suggest, came to be critical to Plato's adventures at Syracuse.

As a third-generation Pythagorean and a Mathematic, Archytas was reared in a Pythagoreanism developing from the charismatic toward the rational. Archytas's politics were both practical and theoretical. One of the few surviving fragments of his writing (frag. 3 in Huffman 2005, 182) makes the link explicit:

> Either by learning from another or by discovering it yourself you must come to know what you did not know. Learning is from someone other than oneself; discovery is by oneself and personal. Discovery without seeking is baffled and rare; by seeking it is available and easy, but without knowledge it is impossible to seek.
>
> Once calculation is discovered it ends conflict and increases concord. When this comes to be there is no taking advantage, there is equality. It is through this that we reach agreement in contracts; through this the poor take from the rich and the rich give to the needy—both trusting through this to have equality. It provides a standard and an inhibitor of the unjust, since it stops those who know injustice from calculation before they act, persuading them that they cannot get away with it whenever they come to that point. And by it the unjust are identified, and so it prevents their injustice.

Thus, the man who refounded mechanics on mathematical principles turned his mind to political economy. The focus is on contracts; by "calculation" (*logismos*), he clearly means, in this context, definite money prices. In the sixth century, Solon made it illegal in Athens to lend money on the security of the family farm or of personal liberty. Archytas, two hundred years later, here seems to be warning against the danger of informal, traditional relations leading to exploitation. Money transactions provide transparency and enforceable agreements.

A passage in Aristotle's *Politics* (1320b) supports this reading of the fragment:

> It is the mark of a kindly and intelligent elite that distributing the poor among themselves they provide start-up capital and thus encourage them to go into business. It is a fine thing to imitate the policies of Taras. Those people shared their property with the poor for the use they could make of it, and thus obtained the good will of the masses. Furthermore they made all the offices of two kinds, some elected, others by lot, those by lot so that the people could have a share in them, the elected ones so that they'd have better government. It is also possible to make the same offices partly by lot, partly elected. So it is explained how a democracy ought to be managed.

Aristotle thus identifies Taras under Archytas as a (moderate) democracy.

Whereas the first-generation Pythagoreans became a political force by their solidarity with each other, by their shared doctrines and secrets and common devotion to a charismatic teacher—and thus, in effect, claimed to replace the old elite with a new elite of the enlightened—the later Pythagoreans evidently saw their political task as the maintenance of harmony between the existing moneyed elite and the rest. They ceased to be conspiratorial without ceasing to be philosophical, but their idea of philosophical government was what Danielle Allen has called "managerial."[25] Archytas was certainly a Pythagorean, and no doubt most of his closest associates were Pythagoreans also—membership in the order continued to be a reliable source of friendship—but their political aims were not the purification of society but moderation through balance.

The Pythagorean name for balance—and what they meant by justice—was, Aristotle tells us, *to antipeponthos* (τὸ ἀντιπεπονθός), which we might define as correspondence or reciprocity of effect or experience (*Ethica Nicomachea* 1132b). This was evidently a term in mechanics, which may suggest a connection to Archytas: Aristotle, discussing the lever, says "the weight that moves is correspondent (*antipeponthos*) to the weight that is moved as are the respective distances from the center, so that the further one is from the fulcrum, the more easily he moves the weight" (*Mechanics*[26] 850b).

In the *Nicomachean Ethics*, Aristotle discusses the political application of this term, remarking that it is not a principle of distributive or corrective justice, and if (as he speculates) it means an eye for an eye, it recommends not justice but injustice. The proper sphere of *to antipeponthos*, he asserts, is voluntary exchange, as in gift exchange or commercial transactions, which are just if "each has his own"—and this is often most conveniently managed through money prices (*Ethica Nicomachea* 1133b). Here Aristotle, employing a Pythagorean term, is evidently developing a Pythagorean idea of a just society. Once again, we can see that the statesman's task would be to manage this order so as to maintain stability.

---

25. The term is used in chap. 8 and 9 of *Why Plato Wrote* (2010), specifically pp. 111, 140, and 141.

26. This work is generally considered to be spurious.

Plato's Second Voyage

In 366 BCE, immediately after Dionysius the Elder died and Dionysius the Younger succeeded him, Dion, as we have seen, took steps to secure his own primary influence with the young tyrant. In this context, Dion sent Plato an invitation—or, rather, an urgent appeal—to come to Syracuse. Plato summarizes this appeal in the *Letter* (327e–328a), mentioning three "inducements": first, that he, Dion, was already a powerful person in this powerful imperial city; second, that he was already the center of a philosophical circle consisting mostly of his own relatives; and third, that the young Dionysius was enthusiastically "always talking about philosophy and education." Such an opportunity was unlikely to recur and must be seized at once before Dionysius fell under other influences.

Why did Plato accept? In the *Letter* (328b–329b), he gives two answers to the question: this was his chance to put his political ideas into practice, and he was bound to Dion by ties of friendship too powerful to ignore. These two reasons were actually linked: his friendship with Dion was a philosophical friendship formed through Plato's teaching that philosophy could make a difference in the world. Not to go, therefore, would be a betrayal of both his disciple and his teachings.

It is probable that Plato wrote the *Republic*—his only Socratic dialogue that speaks of the philosopher-king—before 366, and plausible that Dion had read it. We can imagine Dion quoting the *Republic*; there, Socrates insists to Adeimantus (499c–d) on the crucial (if rare) possibility of philosophical rule "if in powerful circles or royal courts—in their sons or in themselves—should arise the true passion (*erōs*) for true philosophy. . . . That this, mind you, is impossible, I insist makes no sense—or else we'll deserve to be ridiculed for idly speaking a mere daydream." In Syracuse, it seemed that the preconditions for philosophical rule had taken place. So in the *Letter* (328b–c) Plato says: "If ever I were to try to bring about my ideas as to laws and the regime, now would be the moment."

Plato was clear that he was to be there as a teacher: Dion was asking of him "discourse and persuasion—just those means by which . . . you are able to turn young people toward goodness and justice" (328d). Plato seems to have remained somewhat vague as to exactly how the conversion of the young tyrant to philosophy would bring about the transformation of the society; for implementation he put himself, it seems, in Dion's hands. Plato thought, "I only had to succeed in persuading one person, and I would have brought about everything good" (328c). Plato admits, in other words, that he went to Syracuse as a political innocent. He thought that "without slaughter and murder . . . [Dion] could establish a happy and true life for the whole country" (327d). He seems not to have thought through how a happy and true life could be established without slaughter in a country so far from truth and happiness.

Dion, however, was no innocent. He had made himself an important figure in the court of Dionysius the Younger, and he knew that the power of tyrants appears absolute only because it is arbitrary. Tyrants have constituencies that they need to manage, groups whose inevitable discontents threaten to turn into organized opposition. Keeping one constituency contented is liable to increase discontent in another. Furthermore, tyrants require subordinates who are both loyal and competent, but the more competent they are, the more independent they tend to become until eventually they are recruited by the opposition.

What did Dion hope to achieve by inviting Plato? The answer seems obvious from Plato's paraphrase of Dion's invitation; he says that Dion spoke of "how his own nephews and relatives were readily disposed to the message and life I always spoke of, and they were fully competent to bring Dionysius along, so that now, if ever, there was every prospect that it could actually happen: philosophers and rulers of great cities could be the same people (328a)."

In other words, in the court politics of Syracuse, philosophy had become the rallying cry of a faction, a faction centering on Dion and his relatives, and if they could recruit Dionysius to their faction they could, through him, rule the empire.

At this point, it is hard not to think of Taras, the philosopher-ruled state at the other end of Greek Italy. In fact, it is hard to see any good reason why Dion, engaged in a factional struggle in his own city, would not have sought out Archytas as his ally. Archytas does not appear in Plato's narrative until much later; however, it is not hard to suspect that a subtext of Dion's invitation to Plato was the idea that philosophical friendship on the Pythagorean model could cement a bond between Syracuse and Taras and thus unite virtually the whole Greek West. Plutarch indeed says explicitly (citing no source) that along with Dion's repeated appeals and letters from Dionysius himself, there came to Plato appeals from "Italy, from the Pythagoreans" that Plato should "take hold of the young soul led astray by great authority and power, and master him with weighty discourse" (Plutarch, *Dion* 11).

As soon as Plato arrived, however, he found "Dionysius's whole environment full of faction and of slanders made to the tyrant against Dion" (*Letter* 329b). The *Letter* depicts the ensuing struggle as essentially person-to-person, between Plato and Dionysius, with Dion's slanderers in the background. Plutarch's *Dion* (11–12) names another important player:

> Those who were at war with Dion fearing Dionysius's conversion persuaded him to recall Philistus from his exile, a man highly cultivated in rhetoric and fully cognizant of tyrannical manners, with the thought that he would be a counterweight to Plato and philosophy. . . . He was in exile with some guest-friends in Adria, where he is thought to have completed the greater part of his *History*. He never returned during the life of the Elder [Dionysius]. But after his death, as already noted, the envious hatred felt by others toward Dion brought him back, as being someone more serviceable to them and more faithful to the tyranny.
>
> This man on his return was immediately identified with the tyranny. There were others who slandered and accused Dion to the tyrant, saying he was in talks with Theodotus and Heracleides about the dissolution of the tyranny. It seems that Dion did hope that Plato's presence might reduce the arbitrary and overly harsh aspect of the tyranny and make of Dionysius a cautious and law-abiding ruler. If he resisted and did not soften, Dion had decided to depose him and turn the government over to the Syracusans, not that he favored democracy, but that it was altogether better than tyranny for those who could not establish a healthful aristocracy.

In Plutarch's account, the "slanders" were not entirely false; Dion did indeed intend some kind of regime change, and Plato was his intended instrument. Plutarch seems to imply a chronology wherein Philistus's recall was a response to Plato's acceptance of Dionysius's invitation but prior to Plato's arrival. As the struggle for the soul of the young tyrant began, both sides mobilized their intellectual leadership. The contest was thus framed as a skirmish between the historian, for whom politics was about power, and the philosopher, for whom politics was about virtue. Plato thus found himself again facing the man who (apparently) had, as captain of the citadel, sent him home from his first visit on a Spartan ship. Their opposition was later evidently a public matter; when Plato returned to Syracuse for his third visit, Plutarch reports, "Sicily was full of hope . . . that Plato could overcome Philistus, and philosophy, tyranny" (Plutarch, *Dion* 19).

Plutarch gives a highly colored account of Plato's first interactions with Dionysius (*Dion* 13–14):

> When matters were in such a state Plato arrived in Sicily; in their first meeting he met with wonderful affection and respect. An impressively decorated royal chariot was waiting when he got off the trireme, and the tyrant made sacrifice in thanks for the great good fortune which had come to his rule. The restraint of his banquets and the decorum of his court, along with the tyrant's own gentle way of doing business stirred in the citizens wonderful hopes of change. There was a kind of general rush toward discourse and philosophy, and they say the tyrant's palace was full of dust from the number of people drawing geometric diagrams. Within a few days there was a traditional festival in the palace—and when the herald made the usual prayer that the tyranny should endure many years unshaken, Dionysius, who was present, said (we are told), "Won't you leave off cursing us?" This produced plenty of distress in the party of Philistus; they thought that with time and familiarity Plato's power would become unbeatable if on such brief acquaintance the young ruler's judgment could be so altered and transformed.
>
> So their denunciation of Dion was no longer sporadic and secretive, but out in the open; they said Dion couldn't get away with bewitching and poisoning Dionysius with Plato's discourse so that Dionysius would voluntarily abdicate and Dion, picking up the power he laid down, would confer it on Aristomache's sons, his nephews. Some made a point of their disgust if the Athenians, sailing here with a great force on land and sea, had lost it and perished before they took Syracuse, while now these people would depose Dionysius's tyranny by means of a single sophist, conspiring to persuade him to run from his massive bodyguard and his four hundred triremes and his thousands of cavalry and his many times as many heavy-armed men, so that he would seek out some secret good in the Academy and find happiness in geometry, yielding the happiness of power and money and luxury to Dion and his nephews.
>
> As this, beginning with suspicion, was growing into open wrath and faction, a secret letter was brought to Dionysius which Dion had written to the Carthaginian agents, instructing them, when they were in talks with Dionysius concerning the peace, not to make contact without him, because through him they could make everything permanently binding.

> Dionysius read this letter to Philistus and taking Philistus's advice, as Timaeus says, Dionysius beguiled Dion with false words of compromise. He made a pretense of a moderate settlement and said he was merely inviting him from the acropolis to the seaside; then he showed him the letter and accused him of conspiring with the Carthaginians against him. Dion wanted to defend himself but was not heard; rather, just as he was, he was immediately put in a small boat; the sailors were ordered to take him away and land him somewhere in Italy.

Plato's own brief account of these events is as follows: "I supported Dion as far as I was able, which was but little, and after three months or so, Dionysius accused Dion of plotting against the tyranny, put him in a small boat, and sent him off in disgrace" (*Letter* 329b–c). The whole experiment, in other words, lasted only a few months. Plato's presence in Syracuse had been destabilizing; rather than securing Dion's position, it had contributed to making it untenable. Plato's next challenge was to get out of Syracuse.

In Plato's description (*Letter* 329b–330c), this was an entirely personal issue between himself and Dionysius; Plutarch, following Timaeus, expands it to include Philistus. However, Plato and Philistus were not the only intellectual figures at court; Diogenes Laertius tells us that Plato's faithful disciple, Xenocrates, went with him. And there were others.[27]

Patronage of poetry and architecture was already in the sixth century one of the familiar ornaments of Greek tyranny. Polycrates of Samos built temples and aqueducts; he apparently also patronized poets. In the fifth century, Sicilian tyrants patronized Simonides, Bacchylides, Pindar, and Aeschylus; Dionysius the Elder was a patron of poets and himself a poet; at the end of his life, he was awarded a prize at Athens for his tragedy *The Ransoming of Hector*. In the fourth century, as the cultural focus shifted, tyrants and monarchs began to patronize science and philosophy. Thus, we find the astronomer Helikon and Aristippus, the hedonist, among the Socratics and thus Plato's adversary, both at the court of Dionysius. Plutarch (*Dion* 19) again:

> Aristippus of Cyrene was there and remarked that Dionysius's generosity played it safe: he offered them small gifts when they asked for large ones, while he offered much to Plato, who wouldn't take

---

27. See Diogenes Laertius 4.6.

it. . . . Later between Plato and Dionysius . . . there began to be differences concealed from outsiders. . . . Helikon of Cyzikus, one of Plato's followers, predicted an eclipse of the sun; when it happened as he foretold, the tyrant, impressed, presented him with a talent of silver. Aristippus, joking with the other philosophers, said he also could predict an unexpected event. When they asked him to tell it he said: "I foretell that quite soon Plato and Dionysius will be enemies."

The anecdotal evidence, such as it is, tells us that Plato was generally unpopular in Athens and at Syracuse with the other Athenian Socratics; their presence at Dionysius's court evidently was anything but supportive of Plato in his efforts to support Dion—of whom, in any case, they had no reason to be protective.

Plato's situation was, paradoxically, made more difficult by the fact that Dionysius did not become his enemy; on the contrary, he became so attached to Plato that he would not let him leave. "He grew continually fonder of me as time went on . . .—in the sense that he wanted me to praise him rather than Dion and to be his special friend rather than Dion's . . . I stood it all, holding on to the first notion I'd come with, that he might somehow become passionate for the philosophical life. But he held out and beat me" (*Letter* 330a–b). Dionysius eventually seems to have lost interest; he may have been distracted by other matters. Plato mentions that while in Syracuse, he had "brought about guest-friendship and amity between Dionysius and Archytas and his Taras people" (*Letter* 338c), and we may suspect some intervention from that quarter. In any case Dionysius, making various promises he had no intention of keeping, let Plato go. So Plato came home—defeated.

Dionysius was probably genuinely attracted by Plato's extraordinary qualities, even though he was not himself in the least interested in living the philosophical life. But he also may have realized that an open break with Plato could have real-world consequences in the realm of power. Dionysius would have recognized that Plato, however innocent he might be in the ways of the world, was, in his way, a powerful person with his own constituency. Plato had his admirers, and they overlapped with Dion's friends. Dion was a threat to Dionysius, and Plato was one of Dion's assets. It would weaken Dion if Dionysius could detach Plato from Dion. So long, however, as he was unable to separate

Plato from Dion, he was forced to tempt Plato with the hope that he and Dion might reconcile. When he finally agreed to let Plato go, it was with a promise to recall Dion within a year (Plutarch, *Dion* 16). This promise was, of course, not kept.

Dion in Exile

Plutarch (*Dion* 15) tells us that when Dion was sent off in a small boat

> —people thought this harsh and there was grief in the tyrant's household among the women. The city of Syracuse was uneasy, expecting revolutionary events and a quick regime change resulting from the excitement about Dion and the tyrant's general unreliability. Dionysius was aware of this and frightened; he reassured Dion's friends and the women that Dion was not in exile but just gone abroad, so that he [Dionysius] should not be forced by Dion's presence to act mistakenly through anger at his arrogance. He handed over two ships to Dion's household telling them to load in whatever of his property they wanted and to send his servants to Dion in the Peloponnese. Dion's property was great and his lavish furniture and tableware almost on a tyrannical scale; all this his friends collected and sent. Lots more was sent by his women and his followers, enough to make him famous in Greece for his possessions and wealth, so that the affluence of his exile should reflect the power of the tyrant.

From 367 to 357, Dion was in exile. After noting that Dionysius sent Dion his rents (*Dion* 15), Plutarch devotes one section to this period (*Dion* 17):

> Plato once he'd turned him toward philosophy included Dion in the Academy. He resided however with Callipus, one of the members.
> He acquired a farm as a recreation, and later when he sailed for Sicily he gave it to Speusippus as a gift. Speusippus was his best friend in Athens; he dined with him—since Plato wished that through enjoyable company, finding opportunities for modest playfulness, Dion's character would be tinctured with a sense of the pleasurable. Speusippus was just the man for that: Timon in *Silloi* calls him "good at jokes."
> When Plato was assigned to pay for a boy's chorus, Dion took responsibility for the chorus and covered the whole cost out of his pocket. Plato

approved of Dion's seeking public recognition in this way; Plato was more concerned about Dion's being seen favorably than about his own reputation.

Dion went about to the various cities; he relaxed with the best people, the political leaders, and joined their collective rituals, displaying nothing awkward or tyrannical or dissolute in his manners but rather good sense and virtue and courage, graceful in his conversation as to his discourse and his philosophy. In this way he acquired general goodwill and admiration, along with public honors and civic decrees. The Lacedaemonians made him a Spartan citizen, disregarding the anger of Dionysius—even though Dionysius was their faithful ally against the Thebans.

We are told that Dion was once invited to the home of Ptoeodorus of Megara. Evidently Ptoeodorus was a rich and powerful person. When Dion saw a crowd around his doors, a mass of busy people, and that Ptoeodorus was difficult of access and unavailable to them, he glanced at his friends who were disapproving and annoyed and said "Do we find fault with this? Because we ourselves always did such things in Syracuse."

In this rather miscellaneous account, Plutarch evidently draws on several different sources. A number of things are worth noticing. Plato is said to have "turned [Dion] toward philosophy," which probably means that he got Dion to renounce, at least for the time being, his political ambitions and join the community that was the Academy. It does not seem that the Academy (unlike the Pythagorean orders), ever in its history, had defined members or formal admissions; it maintained its original character as a circle of friends joined in admiration of Plato—of his person, and later of his memory. The word I have translated as "members" is in Greek *gnōrimoi*; this originally meant "acquaintances" (as opposed to friends); then it became a political term, and meant "the notables," that is, the people worth knowing from a political point of view. Then in Hellenistic histories of philosophy it acquired a new meaning: those who are taught by a particular philosopher. I have translated the word here in this sense. However, it is notable that in the *Letter* (333d–e), Plato flatly denies that Callippus, who later murdered Dion, was his friend through philosophy rather than just the "regular kind" of friend. Nevertheless, I believe that Plutarch's source identified Callippus as an Academic.

As to the farm, real property in Attica could be owned only by Athenian citizens—unless, as might well have happened in Dion's case, the Assembly had passed a specific decree of *egktēsis* in his favor. The alternative is that while the farm was paid for by Dion, the title was, from the beginning, held by Speusippus. In any case, the property was finally abandoned to him. This is relevant to the question of the funding of philosophy. As the Academy did not have members, so it did not charge tuition (unlike Isocrates's contemporary school); Socrates, who had no visible means of support, was evidently supported by gifts from his friends, and the Academy seems to have inherited such informal funding. This would make Dion, with his great wealth, a particularly valuable associate. A farm, it should be noted, is not only a pleasant place in the country (most prosperous Athenians had one) but also, as occupied by a tenant farmer, a source of income (cf. Xenophon, *Memorabilia* 3.11.4). It is tempting to suspect that this farm became a long-term support of the Academy.

Funding is also relevant to the boys' chorus. To be *chorēgos* (χορηγός) of such a chorus was a tax obligation—evidently, Plato's rather modest fortune was large enough to obligate this not inconsiderable expenditure. (The chorus needed an extended period of training under a professional trainer, as well as costumes, etc.) By picking up the expenses, Dion put money in Plato's pocket.

Then we hear of Dion's travels, particularly to Sparta and Megara. Both of these were, of course, oligarchies, ruled by the "best people" and, as such, opposed to tyranny (but not at all philosophical). Despite Plato's efforts to turn him from politics, Dion seems to have spent much of his exile making connections with the secular elite and no doubt built a base for his eventual return. Evidently Dion made good use of his time in old-world Greece; he was as rich in golden opinions as he was in money income.

Plato's Third Voyage

Then, in 357, Dionysius provoked the crisis by cutting off Dion's rents. Plutarch (*Dion* 18) says:

> In the course of time Dionysius, becoming jealous and fearing the favorable opinions gained by Dion among the Greeks, stopped sending his revenues and handed the property over to hand-picked trustees.

Plutarch dates this event before Plato's third trip to Syracuse, while Plato (*Letter* 344) says that it happened while he was in Syracuse. I tend to resolve this difference in Plutarch's favor because it seems to me that Plato, not Plutarch, has a motive for revising the chronology: Plato does not want Dion's material loss seen as the main motive or even the immediate provocation of his third visit. He would rather stress his other reasons for going. Perhaps this is a difference without a difference since Plato explicitly does say that Dionysius, in his letter of invitation, wrote: "If you will yield to us and come this time . . . the issues around Dion will be settled in whatever way you wish . . . but otherwise nothing will happen as you wish especially as to Dion's affairs" (*Letter* 339b–c). So whatever the chronology, it is clear that Dion's property was being held hostage for Plato's complicity with the tyrant.

Plato, in the *Letter*, is clearly embarrassed that he went once more to Syracuse. He admits, almost explicitly, that to go again was a mistake, and he should have known it. "Fool me once" as we say, "shame on you; fool me twice, shame on me." In his defense, he was (he says) misinformed; he had all kinds of reports that "Dionysius's passion for philosophy has amazingly revived" (*Letter* 338b). Plato says he did not give much weight to these reports, knowing something of the transient philosophical enthusiasms of the young, and so "thought it safer to say a firm goodbye to Dion and Dionysius" (*Letter* 338b–c). However, Plato found himself under intense pressure—not only with respect to Dion's revenues. Archytas and his circle wrote that they would stand security for Plato and that their beneficial relations with Syracuse would be at risk without him.[28] Plato, that

---

28. Plutarch (Plutarch, *Dion* 18) writes that Dionysius put them up to this. Taras, throughout its history, had been occupied with the Iapygians, the indigenes who occupied the Salentine peninsula to her north. In the time of Archytas, however, the focus shifted to the Lucanians, an Italic people pressing southward through the districts west of Taras, arriving at least as far as Paestum. They therefore were a threat to the Greek coastal cities south of Taras: Metapontum, Heraclea, and Croton. These cities formed a league to organize resistance—originally led by Croton, but when that city was taken over by Dionysius the Elder, taken over by Taras.

These events brought Archytas and Dionysus the Younger face to face. It seems unlikely that whatever his idea of philosophy, Archytas could ever have thought the young Dionysius anything but a dilettante. However, Taras needed to cooperate with

is, found himself entangled both in Dion's personal affairs and West-Greek international politics. It was becoming evident that when the philosopher turns to a worldly project, he discovers himself no longer a free agent but constrained by worldly interests.

Plato also realized that he did have some leverage with Dionysius; the tyrant wanted to be known as a man of culture and, in that sense, did value an association with the most notable man of culture of the day. Finally (I suspect), Plato's grandiosity came into play: he knew himself to be a great teacher, and he could not resist the possibility that he might, after all, convert Dionysius. The tyrant sent a trireme to bring Plato to him and, with it, Archedemus, a Pythagorean resident in Syracuse, to add to the pressure. So Plato went—and with him his nephew Speusippus, later Plato's successor as head of the Academy.[29]

In the event, the failure of their project was this time evident almost as soon as Plato arrived. Plato subjected Dionysius to his "test" (of character), which Dionysius signally failed (*Letter* 340b–341a). After that, Plato at Syracuse focused on protecting Dion's material interests. Dionysius exploited Plato's entanglement in these issues; he presented himself as Plato's philosophical disciple and, at the same time, tried to get Plato to take on the role of Dion's guardian, in which capacity he was supposed to accept on Dion's behalf whatever settlement the tyrant should propose (*Letter* 346a–d). Plato was not deceived by these devices, but he tells us (*Letter* 346d–347a) that he realized that if he broke with the tyrant at this point, Dionysius was in a position to convince the world of his version of events and discredit Plato with Dion—and anyway, he was in the tyrant's power, not free to leave. So he stayed.

Remaining in Syracuse, Plato found himself further entangled, this time with the opposition group around Heracleides. Heracleides, like Dion, had held a leadership position under the tyranny, but otherwise, the two men seem to have had next to nothing in common—except their opposition to Dionysius. For the moment, that was evidently enough. During the

---

Syracuse against the Lucanians; therefore, Archytas was one of those who induced Plato to return to Syracuse.

29. Speusippus is not mentioned in the *Letter* but is featured in Plutarch's account (*Dion* 22). As so often, Plutarch does not name his source.

period when Dion was in exile, he and Heracleides were recorded together as *thearodokoi [. . .] Surakoussais*, entertainers of the visitors from Syracuse, in an inscription at Epidaurus (*Inscriptiones graecae* IV², 1 95.39–40).

Heracleides, as the event will show, was clearly sympathetic to democratic institutions while Dion clearly was not. Nor was Plato; nevertheless, Heracleides's people cultivated Plato while he was in Syracuse, hoping that his influence with Dionysius might help Heracleides. Plato did make some efforts in this direction without success (*Letter* 348b–349b); Heracleides, threatened with arrest, managed to escape into Carthaginian territory (and from there made his way to old-world Greece). Meanwhile Speusippus's circle actively organized against Dionysius, and Speusippus himself wrote to Dion, urging him to return (Plutarch, *Dion* 22). The upshot was that Dionysius's enmity to Plato ceased to be covert and became overt. Plato found himself in well-grounded fear for his life; he wrote to Archytas in Taras, and Archytas sent a diplomatic mission, which got Plato out of there.

Dion Returns to Syracuse

Plato met Dion at Olympia, where he was a spectator at the festival; he told Dion his story, and Dion immediately determined to collect an army and "punish Dionysius" (*Letter* 350c). Plato said Dion was free to invite his friends to join but refused to take any part himself in the use of force; he did, however, permit those close to him, including Speusippus, to take part in the enterprise. Plato's account of what happened next is cursory in the extreme, virtually limited to the claim that, whatever the appearances, Dion was not a bad person, and those who killed him were villains. For an account of the aftermath once Plato had done with Syracuse, we are dependent on others, mainly Plutarch and Diodorus Siculus.

Plutarch tells us (*Dion* 22):

> Dion at this point [when his rents were cut off] turned toward war; although Plato stayed out of it—respecting Dionysius's entertainment of him and feeling his age—Speusippus and the rest of his people cooperated with Dion and called upon him to liberate Sicily, stretching out their hands to him and eagerly giving him pledges of support . . . Dion, encouraged by such messages began to recruit mercenaries secretly and

through intermediaries, concealing his intentions. Other political and philosophical people were involved: Eudemus of Cyprus, to whom after his death Aristotle dedicated his dialogue on the soul, and Timonides of Leucas. They introduced to Dion Miltas of Thessaly, who was a seer and had taken part in the activities of the Academy. Of the exiles from the tyranny, who numbered no less than a thousand, only twenty-five joined the expedition; the rest out of cowardice failed him.

Very few from the Academy joined Dion—perhaps only those few mentioned by Plutarch and Callippus, who had been Dion's host in Athens. It took Dion three years to get his forces together. Finally, in the summer of 357, Dion set off with a small force consisting mainly of some 600 mercenaries. He landed on the south coast of Sicily at Heraclea Minoa, since 408 in Carthaginian territory. The Carthaginian commander here was one of Dion's Carthaginian connections, in fact (we are told) his guest-friend; he provided logistical support (Plutarch, *Dion* 25).

Dion's strategy anticipated Garibaldi: he increased his forces with volunteers as he marched toward Syracuse. He had actually brought with him 2,000 sets of hoplite equipment to equip his new soldiers. In the event, his forces increased to some tens of thousands. He got to Syracuse at a time when Dionysius was away, tending his new possessions up the Adriatic; the people of Syracuse greeted Dion's arrival with enthusiasm. Dionysius on his return occupied the citadel on the island, still held by his forces, and proposed to open negotiations, offering very favorable terms. However, when Dion sent him an embassy, he arrested the ambassadors and, unexpectedly opening the gates, sent his mercenaries against the Syracusans. There followed a battle royal, in which Dion fought hard and was wounded, and Dion's mercenaries ultimately prevailed.

At this point Heracleides, arrived with his own expedition, somewhat independently organized (but most probably paid for by Dion [Westlake 1994, 698]): seven triremes and three supply vessels. His arrival immediately provoked a split in the opposition to the tyrant; some wanted Heracleides as commander, others wanted Dion to remain in charge. The division was papered over by Dion's acceptance of Heracleides as *nauarchos*, naval commander, subordinate to himself. The people of Syracuse continued to meet in disorderly assemblies and to form factions.

Now, Philistus arrived with a substantial number of triremes in support of Dionysius, and the people of Syracuse, trained for naval warfare, took over the city's defense from Dion's mercenaries. They were, in fact, victorious in a naval battle in which, or as a result of, Philistus died. Dionysius, having thus lost his best officer, now escaped from Syracuse (getting past Heracleides), leaving the citadel in the hands of his son Apollocrates. Heracleides, blamed for the escape, responded by getting one of his party to call an Assembly to order a redistribution of land. This proposal was opposed by Dion but it passed anyway. And so Dion's property makes another appearance in the story: Dion had no sooner recovered it from the tyrant than he lost it to the democratic forces.

Heracleides then proposed that the Assembly deprive the mercenaries of their pay and choose new officers. The Assembly then elected twenty-five new generals, Heracleides included and Dion excluded. In this way (Heracleides said), they would be free of Dion's severity, he who "wished like a doctor to put the city on an austere and temperate diet" (Plutarch, *Dion* 37). This new government then tried to detach the mercenaries from Dion, offering them Syracusan citizenship (evidently compensation for losing their wages). The mercenaries, however, remained loyal to Dion; there was civil disorder (*Dion* 38), and Dion took his troops off to Leontini—for at least a century Syracuse's adversary. The Syracusans pursued Dion some distance, but after a brief skirmish withdrew (*Dion* 39). Leontini then gave the mercenaries citizenship and their wages as well. Some kind of general council of the Sicilian allies followed, which delivered a judgment that the Syracusans were at fault. The Syracusans paid no attention (*Dion* 40).

Now, Nipsius the Neapolitan arrived with another naval force supporting Dionysius, bringing food and equipment for those besieged in the island citadel. Once again, there was a naval battle, which the people of Syracuse won, capturing four of the tyrant's ships. The Syracusans then celebrated their victory wildly, and Nipsius, seeing his opportunity, opened the gates of the citadel and turned loose Dionysius's garrison, a barbarian mercenary force. "So the sack of the city started, men being murdered, walls pulled down, women and children dragged screaming into the acropolis" (*Dion* 41). There was nothing for it but to send to Leontini for help and to ask Dion to come back.

During a lull, the barbarians withdrew into the island for the night, and the democratic leaders began to urge the people not to admit Dion's forces. However, when the sack resumed the following day, Heracleides, himself wounded, sent his brother and his uncle to urge Dion to hurry. Much of the city was already on fire, but in the event, Dion and his troops were able to push the barbarians back into the citadel and save the city from total destruction (*Dion* 46).

Having thus recovered his authority, Dion faced the question of settling with Heracleides, remarking (according to Plutarch, *Dion* 47) that his long time in the Academy had habituated him to let go of anger and envy and every kind of desire for victory. So Dion pardoned Heracleides and his people.

An Assembly followed in which Heracleides proposed that Dion should be *stratēgos autokratōr*, a general with absolute power (the same title held by the elder Dionysius during his tyranny); the better sort of people supported this, but the crowd loudly objected to Heracleides being deprived of the admiralty, thinking him more democratic than Dion and more influenced by the many (*Dion* 48). Dion consented and gave Heracleides command at sea but opposed those who tried to proceed with the redistribution of land and houses and invalidated the relevant previous decrees. Thus, Dion recovered the title to his lands. It is, of course, by no means clear that the title bestowed on him by the people had given him authority to rescind decrees passed by the Assembly. However, this was not a period of constitutional government.

Heracleides then collected the soldiers and sailors who had sailed with him and went to Messenia; there, he agitated against Dion, claiming that Dion aimed at tyranny. At the same time Heracleides made some secret agreements with Dionysius, then resident in Locri. Dion had to leave Syracuse with his forces to fend off an attacking force, and Heracleides seized the opportunity to sail on Syracuse with the hope of seizing the city. Dion, however, returned in time to fend off Heracleides and his fleet. While these ships were sailing about, they encountered a Spartan named Gaisulos, who informed them that he had come to take charge of the Sicilians, like Gylippos, during the Athenian siege. Heracleides seized on this man as a kind of preventive medicine against Dion and sent a herald to tell the Syracusans to receive their new commander. Dion answered that they had plenty of commanders, and anyway, if a Spartan commander were required, he himself was a naturalized citizen of that place. So Gaisulos thought better of it; he sailed in to reconcile Dion and Heracleides, making them swear mighty oaths, and swearing an oath himself to defend Dion and punish Heracleides for any bad behavior (*Dion* 49).

At this point, the Syracusans demobilized the navy, leaving Heracleides with nothing to command. Plutarch seems to be quoting someone when he says: "There was nothing for it to do, it was expensive, and just caused quarrels among the commanders" (*Dion* 50). The Syracusans rather tightened their siege of the citadel until Apollocrates, supplies running short and his mercenaries acting up, surrendered the fortress with its arms and equipment; loading three ships, he went off with his mother and sisters to his father. So then Dion was reunited with his mother, wife, and son. Having attained the highest power, he moved into the citadel with them and settled into a modest life "as if he were sharing meals with Plato in the Academy" (*Dion* 52). He now held the tyrant's title—*stratēgos autokratōr*—and inhabited the tyrant's citadel, but he lived without any display of tyrannical luxury and grandeur. Plato actually wrote to him that the whole world was watching—and he himself looked to the Academy as his audience and judges (*Dion* 52).

Heracleides, however, continued his opposition. Plutarch (*Dion* 53) tells us that although he was invited to join the governing council, he refused, saying he was a private person and would take his place in the Assembly with the other citizens. There, he attacked Dion, complaining that he had not leveled the walls of the citadel, and that when the people attempted to break open the tomb of Dionysius the Elder and throw away the corpse, Dion would not permit it. Also, Dion had sent for counselors and corulers from Corinth as if the citizens were not worthy (*Dion* 53).

> Dion really did send for Corinthians, since he hoped that with their presence he could more easily establish the constitution he had in mind. He had in mind to abolish absolute democracy, thinking it no constitution but rather a supermarket of constitutions (as Plato says [*Republic* 557d]). . . . He expected Heracleides to be the main opposition to all this, so while he had long been holding back people who wanted to kill Heracleides, at this point he gave way to them. They went into his house and killed him. The people of Syracuse were sorely grieved by his death; all the same Dion gave him a fine funeral, and along with his army followed the coffin in procession, and then addressed the people. So they came to understand that it was not possible for the city to achieve tranquility if Dion and Heracleides were both to lead the polity.

That is the story as Plutarch tells it; clearly, he is drawing on a source favorable to Dion. (I have left out his numerous and cloying praises of Dion's virtue and the almost as numerous and rather nasty dispraises of Heracleides's bad character.)[30] The murder of Heracleides evidently was the blackest mark on Dion's political career—Plutarch (*Dion* 56) speculates that Dion thought it "a spreading stain on his life and actions." The event is notably absent from the *Letter*. Plutarch's source also seems to have done his best to display it as unavoidable. Yet even from this narrative, it is possible to reconstruct a more positive picture of Heracleides as a man doing his best to make democracy work in Syracuse, and who opposed Dion on principled grounds. Dion evidently decided that Heracleides was all too likely to be successful in his opposition and had to be terminated.

Then Dion himself was murdered by some of the mercenaries he had brought with him from Zakynthus. The motives of these men are obscure, as is Dion's vulnerability. Plutarch (*Dion* 57) says that many were involved in the conspiracy and that many of Dion's people were with him, but none was willing to protect him. Nepos, who seems in this part of the *Life of Dion* (sec. 7) to be following a source hostile to Dion,[31] says that to pay his mercenaries, Dion had recourse to confiscations and thus alienated the landowners who had been his supporters. All agree that the assassination was organized by Callippus (Nepos calls him Callicrates), Dion's Athenian friend. Callippus's motives are also obscure—perhaps simply to take control of Syracuse. In any case, he did so and held the city for thirteen months, driving out the "friends of Dion," who took refuge in Leontini. From there they took part in the displacement of Callippus by Hipparinus, the son of Dion's sister. Hipparinus ruled for two years, and his brother ruled for five years after him. Evidently, this was the period during which Plato wrote his *Letter* to the friends of Dion—or else whoever wrote it placed it then; in any case, Hipparinus is mentioned in the first paragraph. Thus, the project of which Dion was accused even before Dionysius the Elder died— that

---

30. Probably he is following Timonides, who, we remember, came with Dion on his expedition and is known to have written an account of it.
31. Probably Athanis, who completed Philistus's *History*.

Aristomache's children should be the tyrant's heirs—was actually (briefly) achieved after Dion's death.

Dion was intelligent, valiant, and an effective leader. Why did he fail? The sources emphasize his manners, which, despite his successes, left him increasingly isolated. He evidently had what we call an "authoritarian personality": rigid, self-righteous, unable to tolerate criticism or opposition. No doubt he did intend to reform the constitution of Syracuse in the direction of a moderate oligarchy, but the precondition of reform, it seems, was that his will should be law. He was not self-indulgent in the sense of pleasure-loving, but his riches were dear to him: they represented power. This made him the leader and the instrument of the landlord class. His enemies asked: "Why should we be rid of a drunken tyrant only to have a sober one?" (Plutarch, *Dion* 34). Possibly, if he could have let go of his lands, he could have retained his moral authority and become a kind of Syracusan Pericles, of whom Thucydides (2.65) says, "in name it was a democracy, but in fact the rule of one man." Or Dion could have found a model closer to home: Archytas. Taras, however, seems to have been receptive to a certain kind of moderately philosophical autocracy; Syracuse was a uniquely intractable problem.

The next phase belongs to Timoleon of Corinth (Plutarch also wrote his biography); he finally expelled Dionysius from West Greece to exile in Corinth and established a constitutional government in Syracuse—until the next tyrant. But that is another story.

Plato's Politics

In the *Letter* (326b), Plato says:

> The peoples of mankind will never cease from evils until the race of true and proper philosophers arrive at political power, or the powerful persons in the cities through some divine dispensation really philosophize.

He had evidently reached this conclusion or was at least toying with it when he wrote the *Republic*, where Socrates says (473c–d):

> Unless the philosophers rule in the cities or the powerful philosophize legitimately and adequately, and this becomes one single thing: political power and philosophy, and the various talents are necessarily confined within the variety of current pursuits, there will be no cessation of evils for the cities, dear Glaucon, nor as I think for the human race.

The rule of philosophers, then, is the precondition of a better politics, and this precondition, Socrates insists, is itself, while unlikely, yet possible (499b–c):

> That those few philosophers who are not worthless, though generally called irrelevant, should be subjected to some chance necessity to take charge of the city whether they will or not, and the city to obey them, or that the sons of the powerful or the powerful themselves from some kind of divine providence should fall in love (*erōs*) with true philosophy—that either or both of these things are impossible, I see no reason for that.

Furthermore: "One man will be enough, if he has a city that obeys him, to bring to pass all that now is unbelievable" (*Republic* 502b). Here again there is an echo in the *Letter*: "I only had to succeed in persuading one person, and I would have brought about everything good" (328c).

In *Republic* V, nothing is said of tyrants; the tyrant is saved for *Republic* IX, where he is painted in the darkest possible colors: he is the most unhappy of men, and his city is the most unhappy city. When Plato comes back to this theme in the *Laws* (709e–710b), however, the tone is different and the language more explicit:

> "Well now, lawgiver," we shall say to him, "what are we to give you and what kind of a city, so when you get that you will be in a position by yourself to provide for the city an adequate constitution?"
> And what is the correct thing to be said next?
> You mean by the lawgiver?
> Yes.
> As follows: "Give me a city ruled by a tyrant," he will say. "Let the tyrant be young, with a good memory, teachable, with a brave and generous nature. Also what we earlier said was a necessary element of all virtues, let these be included in the composition of the tyrant's soul, if his talents are to be of any use.

> It seems to me, Megillus, that our guest is saying moderation (*sōphrosynē*) must enter into the composition. Am I right?
> Just the common-or-garden kind, Cleinias, not as someone with the air of revealing a higher truth (*semnunōn*) might declare that moderation is something intellectual, but the kind we already see in children and animals: some have a natural disposition toward intemperance in their pleasures, and some toward temperance. In the absence of tempting so-called goodies that are not worth much. You know what I mean, I suppose.

This text may have something to tell us about how Plato, considering Dion's summons, conceived himself as active in Syracuse: he and Dion would be in the role of the lawgiver, teaching good policy to a pliant ruler. Here was a chance for political action that did not require the acquisition of power: power was already in the hands of someone (according to Dion) educable. The *Laws* was written after Plato's Syracusan adventure, and in that context the passage is clearly ironic: be careful what you ask for. Nevertheless, it may carry a kind of nostalgia for Plato's moment of hope. There may also be here a touch of rueful regret: "I forgot to ask about his temperance and moderation."

On the following page (711d–712a), the *Laws* has something to say about the reform of politics:

> When a divine passion (*erōs*) for a moderate and just manner of life springs up in certain great and powerful people, powerful under a monarchy or through being distinguished through superiority of wealth or birth. . . . This is the same story in respect to any kind of power, that when the greatest power comes to a person through his intelligence and moderation, that is the natural origin of the best polity with laws to match, and there is no other way it can ever happen.

This, I take it, is Plato's theory of political reform: nothing can improve the state except the virtue of the rulers; virtue then can be distributed from the top down as subjects come to imitate their superiors. If this theory is not explicitly stated in the *Letter* (although it is pretty clearly implied at 335c–e), that, no doubt, is because it was taken to be self-evident.

There are three places in the *Letter* where Plato offers a partial statement of his political principles. The first is the comparison of the political consultant to the physician (*Letter* 330c–331d): no right-thinking doctor would give advice concerning health to a patient who refused to abandon an unhealthy way of life; the same principle applies to a government. In fact, Plato asserts that "when someone seeks my counsel concerning some critical issue in his life, for example concerning getting money or the care of his body or his soul; if I think him in some kind of shape in his daily life or that he will take my advice in the matter about which he consults me, I give my advice with a whole heart" (*Letter* 331a–b)—and it is just the same with a city. Plato explicitly praises Dion's willingness to accept this principle; he "was ready to live the rest of his life better than the rest of the Italians and Sicilians, embracing virtue rather than pleasure and luxury in general" (*Letter* 327b).

The second passage, immediately following the first and already quoted, is Plato's praise of friendship as the source of political stability. He and Dion became friends, and they together tried to show Dionysius the strength and reliability of this sort of friendship (*Letter* 332d):

> Once he was set on the right path, he was to acquire new friends from among his relatives and of his own age, friends in harmony with him as to virtue. Most of all he should make friends with himself because he was wonderfully lacking in that—we didn't say this explicitly, it wasn't safe, but we hinted at it and armed ourselves with arguments about how men in general could make secure themselves and those who might follow them, while everything would turn out in the opposite way if he did not go in that direction.

We know from Plato's comments on Callippus (*Letter* 333d–e) that he thinks the only trustworthy friendship is philosophical friendship, and it was surely this kind of friendship that they had in mind for Dionysius.

Clearly, both of these principles are to be adopted by the social elite, which in the reformed Syracuse, as in every Greek city, was to constitute the political class. Plato explicitly speaks of giving political advice "whether one man rules or several" (*Letter* 330d)—he does not propose to advise the multitude, who in any case have limited access to "pleasure and luxury in general." So politics is to be founded on a temperate elite, who in their common pursuit of virtue will form strong friendships; within this, there is to be an inner elite of the philosophers whose friendship alone will be unshakeable.

How was this to be accomplished by converting the tyrant to philosophy? Presumably, a temperate elite would form around the tyrant by imitation of his goodness, his setting aside pleasure in favor of the pursuit of virtue. Tyrants, who hold (in principle) a monopoly of resources, find their subjects highly motivated to imitate them.

The inclusion of the tyrant in a web of philosophical friendship would arise of necessity from his own philosophical commitments and would assure him of a trustworthy constituency. It seems not to have occurred to Plato (although it surely occurred to Dion) that when the philosophers became the tyrant's inner circle, those outside it would perceive them as a faction who had conquered political power. No doubt, from Dion's point of view, that would have been all to the good; his people would enjoy the advantages and prestige of the winners, and they deserved it.

It is sometimes assumed that Plato's aim at Syracuse must have been to establish, through Dionysius, a polity something like that described in Plato's *Republic* (although the *Letter* says nothing of the kind). This is no place to attempt an analysis of the *Republic*; suffice it to say that, in my view, there is no stable account in the *Republic* of the best polity. Rather, Socrates takes his interlocutors through an educational process, including a series of somewhat inconsistent utopian speculations. This process leaves them with some idea of the meaning of a liberal education and the possibility of ethical maturity. The passage in the *Republic* actually most relevant to Plato's hopes for Syracuse would be where Socrates is assuring Adeimantus that the people will accept the authority of the philosophers once they realize that philosophers want nothing for themselves and care only for truth and virtue—although it may be necessary to purify the city first before the philosophers attempt to rule (*Republic* 449b–501c). This notion of a preliminary purification, though rather vaguely stated in the *Republic*, seems to imply the position of *Letter* 330c–331d (already discussed), the analogy between political reform and medical treatment—so that Adeimantus is being told that the people will accept the philosophers' authority to the extent that the people—the best people—have already given up honor, wealth, and pleasure as primary goals and have abandoned their competition for obtaining these things. In other words, philosophical rulers will be acceptable to people who have already made an ethical commitment to philosophy.

Plato, in the *Letter*, then, holds to his conviction that a virtuous philosopher—such as Dion—would be the best of rulers and create the best of polities; his experience in Syracuse, however, has shown him that such a man, at least at Syracuse, cannot obtain power, or if he obtains it cannot hold it. So his third piece of political advice, his counsel to Hipparinus and the "friends of Dion" after Dion's death, is to convene a constitutional convention of fifty highly respectable (and appropriately compensated) men who will disinterestedly write new laws for Syracuse (*Letter* 337b–e). This plan would surely have resulted in a moderate oligarchy. By the date of the *Letter*, this was the most old-fashioned Greek model of good government. It was still working in some places but had never been made to work in Syracuse—for any length of time.

At the end of the *Letter* (351a–c), Plato becomes explicit about the alternatives to a moderate well-led oligarchy:

> Dion's intention was just what I would say mine should be—or that of any moderate person—as to his own resources and friends and as to the city, namely he would intend by conferring all the benefits in his power thereby to reach the highest position in the highest offices. This is not to be done by enriching oneself and comrades and city through plots and pulling together conspiracies, out of poverty and lack of self-control, overcome by helplessness in the face of pleasure, going on to execute the property owners—calling them "enemies"—and then to hand out their wealth to one's collaborators and comrades telling them that no one should say it's their fault if people find themselves poor. It's all the same if one becomes popular with his city through this kind of benefaction, passing decrees to redistribute to the many what belongs to the few, or takes charge of a great city, which controls many smaller ones, then redistributes to his own city what belongs to the smaller, with no kind of justice.

Plato here rejects what we nowadays call a "kleptocracy"—to the victors belong the spoils—and the kind of populism represented at Syracuse by Heracleides, as well as imperial taxation, presumably of the sort extorted by the fifth-century Athenian Empire. While he insists that avarice and self-indulgence are the cause of misgovernment, he remains clear that the security of property, no doubt particularly inherited property, is the foundation of civic justice. Thus, while he evidently foresaw that the invasion of

Syracuse would come to nothing but trouble, he remained sympathetic to Dion's determination to overcome the man who had stolen his birthright.

In any case, there is now no more talk of philosophy. It is something like what Dion attempted when he called in some Corinthians, and it is something like what Timoleon actually achieved. So it seems that, at least at Syracuse, Plato's idea of the best government proved, as Socrates is made to suspect in the *Republic* (499c), "a mere daydream."

Plato's Philosophy

Plato as Author

Of all the abuses he suffered at the tyrant's hands, Plato in the *Letter* (341b–342a) is angriest about Dionysius's claim to have learned Plato's philosophy and even to have written a book about it—

> not anything I told him; I know nothing of those things. I know there are some others who have written on these same things, but who in the world they are, they themselves don't even know. This is what I have to say to all those who have written and will write about what matters to me, whether they have heard it from me or from others or have discovered it themselves. In my view these people have no command of the thing.
>
> Nor is there now nor will there ever be any composition of my own about these things—because it cannot be put into words like other objects of study, but from long companionship concerned with the thing and from living with it, suddenly as when a fire leaping across kindles a light, it comes to be in the soul and from that time maintains itself. And I know this, that if it were written or verbalized by me it would be done best—and when it's done badly, I'm as pained as anyone. If I thought it could be adequately written for the many and put into words, what would be a finer way for us to pass our lives than to write up such a great boon to mankind and bring its nature into the light for all? But I think even the attempt to verbalize it is no good, except for some few who are able to find it themselves with minimal instruction; in the case of others it fills some with an unearned sense of superiority, and others with a sublime and hollow hope, as if they'd learned something really awesome [*semna*].

Here, the *Letter* digresses from narrative and counsel; Plato indirectly gives an account of his own work. Now, the question of authenticity becomes acute because, at this point, the *Letter* directly affects our interpretation of the aspect of Plato we most care about, namely, his writings. If Plato wrote these words, we can hardly disregard them; if he did not, then (as I said) they were written by someone who has considered his work, who possibly had personal knowledge of the author, and who is, in any case, a lot closer to Plato than we are. So they deserve our consideration.

In the first place, the *Letter* insists that we take seriously the passage on writing in the *Phaedrus* (275d–e).

> This writing, Phaedrus, has a strange quality, rather like portrait painting. Its productions stand before us as if they were alive, but if you ask them something, they preserve a very dignified silence. It's the same with verbal compositions. You might think they have something intelligent to say, but if you ask them something in your wish to understand what they said, they just send always the same message. So when someone has once written it, the same statement rolls about everywhere the same for those who understand it and identically for those unfitted for it; it does not know whom it should talk to and whom not. When it is distorted and unjustly insulted it always has to call on its father for help—because it cannot defend or help itself.

As it stands, this speaks merely of the need for individual instruction: only one-to-one can the teacher correct misunderstandings, respond to objections, and give examples from the student's own experience; only in this way can theory and doctrine enlist the power of personal connection.[32] This is a warning against book learning, or more precisely, publication. The *Letter*, however, says that Plato's philosophy cannot be put into words at all. The infamous "philosophical digression" (342a–344d) is an (admittedly somewhat awkward) attempt to say why this is so.[33]

---

32. The *Statesman*'s critique of law at 294a–297b also contains an emphasis on individual instruction, but tends toward the *Letter*'s more general critique of writing with its assertion that its rigidity makes it inadequate to describe the instability of human affairs.
33. See Sayre (1988) for a similar argument that the philosophical digression is a critique of any attempt to verbalize philosophy, orally or in written form. However, Sayre comes to different conclusions about how we should view the dialogues in light of this. See

What is put into words, then, is not philosophy but something else, something less serious (*spoudaios*). This also is in the *Letter* (344c–d):

> Whenever you see someone producing written work, either the laws of a lawgiver or in any other form whatsoever, these are for him evidently something not particularly serious even though he himself is a serious person, while *those* things he laid away in the best part of himself—but if he really in all seriousness committed his thoughts to writing, "then, you know, they"—not gods, but mortals—"took away his wits."

These are the words of a writer, and this is a puzzle—just as Socrates in the *Phaedrus* appears to be indicting Plato, even though Socrates's words were written and published by Plato. In the *Phaedrus* (276a–e) Socrates immediately resolves the contradiction:

> Socrates: There is discourse . . . which comes with knowledge, written in the soul of the student, able to defend itself, and knowing those to whom to speak and with whom to keep silence.
> Phaedrus: You mean the living and animate discourse of the knower; written discourse may justly be called the image of this.
> Socrates: Absolutely. [Here I elide two of Phaedrus's responses and the simile of writing to the gardens of Adonis, little plants ritually planted in small pots, and expected to wither.] But these gardens in writing, as it seems, he will sow and write as a form of play, when he does write, treasuring up reminders for himself, when he shall come to forgetful old age, and for any other who is following the same track, and he will enjoy watching their delicate growth. Whenever others are enjoying other amusements, getting drunk at banquets and such things, then this man, as is likely, will instead spend his time in the amusement I describe.
> Phaedrus: This is a very noble amusement you compare with trivialities, Socrates, of the man who is able to play with discourse, making up stories about justice and the other things you talk about.
> Socrates: That is true, my dear Phaedrus.

Metcalf (2019) for the argument that the philosophical digression is primarily a critique of "syngrammatic writing," taking Plato's dialogues to represent an alternative form of writing that would live up to the standards of the "soul-writing" in the *Phaedrus*. Both authors stress the importance of the practice (*epitēdeuma*) of philosophy in community.

The *Dialogues*, it seems, are fiction. (Phaedrus calls them *mythoi*, "stories.") Socrates's repeated victories, as dramatized here, demonstrate the power of philosophy, but only fictionally, where you are allowed to make up your facts and make the story come out any way you like. They do not teach Plato's philosophy—except, perhaps, in the modified way that we can recognize in a good story something we already knew.

It is generally agreed that Plato was a great imaginative artist. We do not deny his greatness if we accept that the *Dialogues* were not his serious work. He could indeed have seen the Academy as his real work and the *Dialogues* as relaxation, like dinner parties. From the point of view of his philosophy, the *Dialogues* are fiction.

Fiction is not serious because it does not have to be true. If a work of fiction has a message, it can always prove its point because the authors are allowed to invent their facts. Aristotle tells us that this distinguishes fiction from history. History is faced with facts: "What Alcibiades did and what happened to him" (Aristotle, *De arte poetica* 1451b11). Fiction is a game of "what if?" speculation worked out persuasively. If fiction is successful, all the facts fit together in a meaningful way, and we say this "makes sense." Aristotle calls this a "universal." We go to fiction because it makes more sense than life, and in this way, even though it is inherently unreliable, fiction interprets life.

To consent to Plato's insistence that the *Dialogues* are not serious—not a way of communicating his philosophy, less like teaching than an alternative for going to dinner parties—does not mean that they are philosophically unimportant. They are by Plato, and they are about philosophy. It does mean that they are virtually useless as sources of history. The *Dialogues* are historical fiction. Almost everyone mentioned in them is a real person, known by their own names. (Callicles has never been securely identified, and Diotima is an obvious invention.) Socrates obviously was a real person, and the *Dialogues* can be read (among other things) as a prolonged meditation on the one fact about him that is securely attested: his trial, conviction, and execution. Otherwise, the historical Socrates can hardly be reconstructed. Clearly, he was a notorious intellectual; Aristophanes is sufficient evidence for this. Evidently, he attracted a circle of friends to whom he was influential; the *Phaedo* (59b–c) provides an incomplete, possibly inaccurate list of those who were present at his death—twelve names plus Crito (present later), besides three others (including Plato himself) who would be expected to be present but were not. A number of these men appear elsewhere in the *Dialogues*, but Plato has shaped them to his purpose. We have no reliable evidence for how, what, or even *where* the historical Socrates taught; Plato and Xenophon represent him very differently, and if we had the dialogues of Antisthenes and Aeschines Socraticus, we would probably have two more contrasting representations.

Plato, in the *Letter*, calls the Socrates he knew the person least fit for the charge of impiety; he remembers the historical Socrates as exceptional in avoiding his own idea of impiety. Socrates obeyed what we might call his moral compass; he refused to do anything he judged wrong. The best evidence for this is his refusal at all three stages of the process against him—the charge, the trial, and the execution—to accept exile as an alternative to death. In the *Dialogues*, however, he is something more; he is represented as the ideal philosopher. His moral compass is in these texts guarded by the *daimonion*, the voice in his head that holds him back when he is about to do something wrong. Furthermore, the *daimonion* only speaks for the negative and is completely reliable; if it says nothing, Socrates knows he is in the right.

It is, of course, possible that the historical Socrates heard advice from an inner voice; in Xenophon (and in the *Theages*, a dialogue uncertainly attributed to Plato) the *daimonion* gives positive advice. Plato's presentation of it is, then, an idealization. Idealization is a kind of simplification and is typical of fiction. Fiction makes more sense than life because it is simpler; events are traced to specific causes, by a kind of thought experiment.

Plato's "what if?" question, I am suggesting, was this: What if the ideal philosopher had taught in fifth-century Athens (as that is reimagined)? How would that go? He would, of course, (like the historical Socrates) attract a large audience, some part of whom would understand him. The intellectual context of the fifth century, however, is also simplified in these texts. Plato's Socrates converses with public figures, never with Chaerephon or any of those identified in the fourth century as Socratics. Even in the *Phaedo*, where many of these are in the audience, the controversy is with two Pythagoreans. This is as close as he gets to anyone who might be worthy of his philosophical respect—not including, for example, Democritus, who is mentioned nowhere in Plato.

Socrates's main adversaries in the *Dialogues* are the sophists, particularly Gorgias and Protagoras. These are represented as unequivocal about their educational aims: they prepare young men for successful worldly—which is to say, political—careers. That was the program adopted and vigorously defended by Plato's life-long educational rival, Isocrates. We hear about the rivalry entirely from Isocrates, but on that evidence, it was absolute. It is reasonable to suppose that Plato's representation of the sophists is his reply in this fictional mode to Isocrates. It would follow that Plato's Socrates's words about Isocrates in the *Phaedrus* (278e–279b)—while hopeful in the context of the dramatic date of the dialogue—as of the date of composition are ironic, with the pathos of hope disappointed. Historical fiction, like any historical narrative—even one constrained by facts—is always in two periods: the period where the story is set and the period in which it is composed. Reimagining the past is the writer's privilege.

The clearest link between Plato's teaching and his *Dialogues* is the *elenchos*. On the evidence of the *Letter*, "friendly refutations" (344b) were Plato's own way of teaching philosophy; in the *Dialogues*, these are the Socratic method. We are told he was famous for them; Meno, in his dialogue, says that before he met Socrates, he had heard of the paralysis caused by talking with him (*Meno*, 80a).

Plato as Teacher

Philosophy can, however, evidently somehow be acquired from a teacher. Plato knew he had made this happen with Dion, certainly, and with others. In the *Letter*, he imagines Dion bringing up against his hesitation to enter the Syracusan arena the potential of Plato's "discourse and persuasion— just those means by which . . . you are able to turn young people toward goodness and justice and settle them in mutual friendship and alliance" (328d). The only precondition is that the student understands the difficulties and freely accepts them. This is the point of the "test"—which Plato had evidently administered before (340b–341a).

Later in the *Phaedrus* (276e–277a), Socrates is more specific about the "living word"; it happens whenever:

> someone employs the art of dialectic, taking a soul suited to it, and there cultivates and sows discourse along with knowledge, discourse able to come to its own help and that of the cultivator, not fruitless but bearing seed, whence others being planted in other personalities are able to

accomplish this and so make it immortal, and which make their possessor happy to the degree this is possible for mortals.

The *Phaedrus* does not have much to say about the art of dialectic other than that it employs collection and division. In the *Letter* (344a–c), where Plato talks mostly about philosophical asceticism, he does have a little more to say about dialectic and its relation to talent:

> If someone is not akin to the business, no skill of apprehension or memory will make him so—the starting point cannot be found in conditions alien to it—so that those who are not adapted or akin to what is fine in the case of justice or anything else, although in other matters they have apprehension and memory—nor those who are akin, but lack apprehension and memory—neither of these will ever learn the truth of virtue so far as it can be learned—nor of vice either. The falsehood and the truth of every reality must be learned together, with constant practice over a long period, as I said when I began. With difficulty in joint practice of these things in each case, names and definitions, appearances and perceptions, being refuted in friendly refutations, employing question and answer without ill will, then understanding shines forth in each case and intuition, focused to the furthest degree humanly possible. That is why no one who is serious about serious things will ever write and thus create a basis for human ill will and bafflement.

But refutations, *elenchoi*, are a large part of the content of the *Dialogues*. So it appears that while the *Dialogues* cannot teach philosophy, they can represent aspects of philosophical teaching. It is only that in the *Dialogues*, refutation is seldom friendly—although there are exceptions, for example, Socrates's talk with Polemarchus in *Republic* I—and this, of course, is intended by Socrates to provoke the conflict with Thrasymachus. Evidently, Plato understood that the soul of drama is conflict. An extended imitation of live consensual dialectic, with all its fits and starts, would be hopelessly boring and tend to discredit philosophy. The *Dialogues* more often display Socrates's victories—although these, realistically, are marginal: Protagoras compliments Socrates and breaks off the conversation, Callicles wavers, Euthyphro and Hippias are made uncomfortable.

The keyword in the above passage is *elenchos*, given here the usual English translation of "refutation." The Greek word is, however, more specific; it is dialectical, that is, "employing question and answer." An *elenchos* is something like the cross-examination of a hostile witness: a series of leading questions that force the interlocutor unwillingly to agree—or to remain silent. It is inherently adversarial. "Friendly refutations" is, therefore, an oxymoron, a claim that the *elenchos* can be transformed in a philosophical context. It seems that philosophical friendship is not only the result of philosophical education but also the precondition of the effective use of *elenchos* in philosophical teaching.

The passage just quoted follows the much-debated philosophical digression—rather tentatively introduced: "Now it comes into my head ... maybe what I'm trying to say would be clearer. ... There is a certain true statement ... I've said it many times" (*Letter* 342a). This is the only surviving prose that is (or purports to be) a sample of Plato's personal instruction. As such, many readers have found it strangely disappointing. We should note, however, that he frames it as his usual answer to the question: Why don't you write out your philosophy or at least explain it in a straightforward manner? The answer is intended to be disappointing: "Because I can't—and no one else could either."

The digression makes a distinction between five things. The first three are objects of thought: name, definition, and representation. The fourth is the modes of thought: knowledge (*epistēmē*), true opinion (*alēthēs doxa*), and intuition (*nous*). The fifth is that "which is knowable [*gnōston*] and truly exists" (*Letter* 342a–b). What is striking about this formulation of what we call Plato's idealism is this: in the *Dialogues*, knowledge is distinguished from right opinion, but here, the two are classed together, along with intuition—in the previous sentence, *epistēmē* is treated as a general term for all three modes of thought (while name, definition, and representation are the " things through which knowledge (*epistēmē*) of [each thing that is] comes to be" (ibid.). Though *nous* is included with the other two, he later says about the fourth: "intuition [*nous*] comes nearest in similarity and kinship to the fifth" (*Letter* 342e). There follows an account of two kinds of conversation (*Letter* 343c–e):

> So long as through comfortable idleness we have not acquired the habit of seeking the truth but are satisfied with whatever images present themselves, we shan't make each other ridiculous, answering questions we are asked, although the questioners are able to tear apart the four and refute us. But whenever we are compelled to answer with the fifth and

clarify it, any capable person who wants to can win, and make most of the audience think—of anyone who expounds in words or in writing or in his answers—that he doesn't know what he's writing or talking about; they are unaware that sometimes the soul of the author or writer is not refuted, but rather the nature of the four in each case, since they are fundamentally inadequate. But a long-term commitment to all this, traversing the upside and downside of each thing, can with labor bear knowledge [*epistēmē*] when talent teaches talent.

In this place, *epistēmē* is used for the understanding that can result from a philosophical education. I conjecture that this explains the inclusion of *nous* along with *epistēmē* above. The light that dawns as the spark passes must be some kind of knowledge, although it is different from the knowledge transmitted by *mathēmata* or *technē*. It is different from what is usually called *epistēmē* and could surely be better described as some kind of *nous*—not Aristotle's kind of *nous*, the foundational ability to understand the definitions and axioms, but rather the culmination of philosophy—not before study but beyond study.

The passage just quoted distinguishes two kinds of *elenchos*. Both proceed by question and answer, and both are aporetic, reaching no kind of satisfactory solution. The first type goes by the specific name of "eristic." This is a kind of game, ideally played before an audience, in which the questioner makes ingenious use of what Plato calls in the *Letter* "the weakness of language" (342e) to make the interlocutor agree to clearly ridiculous conclusions. (Plato's representation of eristic is in the *Euthydemus*.) The questioner gets credit for ingenuity, but the interlocutor is not really puzzled or embarrassed because all parties know that what presents itself as cogent argument is really merely wordplay.

The other type of *elenchos* takes on interlocutors who believe that they understand their own core commitments and know how to defend them. Failure to succeed against a powerful line of questioning leaves the interlocutors uncertain and often angry. This sort of *elenchos* can become the *askēsis* of philosophy if it generates a hunger for more of the same in the form of a shared commitment to the search for truth. This becomes a philosophical friendship. In this search, over time, *aporia* can lead—not to effective and sound arguments but—to *nous*, an intuitive grasp of that reality which cannot be expressed in language.

Be that as it may, so far the *Letter* has shown us four things about philosophy (besides the fact that it is not to be found in published work); all these are echoed in the *Dialogues*, especially the *Phaedrus*. In the first place, philosophy is fundamentally a *passion*; Socrates, in the *Dialogues* speaks several times of an *erōs* for truth and virtue. This passion can lead to a *commitment*, shown in the form of a somewhat ascetic manner of life. This manner of life becomes the basis for a specific type of *friendship*. Then, within the security provided by the mutual trust of the parties, an apparently adversarial process becomes a cooperative *activity*. This activity evidently may be accompanied and supported by study of mathematical sciences. The passage in the *Letter* on the "test" briefly alludes to *mathēmata*, which we may translate as "sciences"—these are laid out in extenso in *Republic* VI. They are propaedeutic to philosophy, not part of its essence, although probably a necessary part of progress toward the goal. And they need not precede dialectic, on the evidence of the *Lysis* that can start on the first day.

The promised goal is that "understanding shines forth in each case and intuition, focused to the furthest degree humanly possible" (*Letter* 344b). Something like this kind of outcome is also presumed in the *Dialogues*, in the recurrent metaphor of ascent, most notably in Diotima's ladder and in the ascent from the Cave in the *Republic*. Philosophy goes beyond, to a higher consciousness.

Beyond the activity there is a goal, a *telos*, referred to in the *Letter*: "Suddenly as when a fire leaping across kindles a light, it comes to be in the soul and from that time maintains itself" (341, already quoted). Also, he says, "a long-term commitment to all this, traversing the upside and downside of each thing, can with labor bear knowledge when talent teaches talent" (343e). And, "there is no danger of anyone forgetting it, once he's got it in his soul; it's as brief as can be" (344d–e).

Here, the *Letter* makes explicit something that is at most implicit in the *Dialogues*. They may be taken only to mean that this higher state is a momentary flash of insight—memorable perhaps, life-changing even, but evanescent. Here, more than anywhere, again, we should like to know whether the *Letter* is Plato himself speaking or an interpreter of his written work. The point is not so important for our understanding of the *Dialogues*, but it does affect how we understand the Academy. The *Letter* makes it clear that this higher reality, when achieved, eventuates in a lasting transformation of the soul. The usual modern term for such a thing is "enlightenment." Of course no one really knows much about enlightenment except the persons who have achieved it, and all they can tell us is that they can't tell us much of anything about it. This, it seems, is what the *Letter* means when it speaks of "the weakness of language." But we can at least say that if the long-term aim of the Academy was, at least originally, to enable persons to reach enlightenment, then its focus was less what we might call philosophy and more a kind of religion or spirituality.

Plato's Religion

Plato's myths are infused with the kind of material we call "Orphic"—a rather unspecific term for a religious tendency, still relatively recent in Plato's time (it can hardly be traced before the early sixth century BCE), alternative or supplementary to the established religion of the Olympian gods. Cults of this type focused on the soul of the individual rather than the welfare of the group; in fact, they accompanied or even brought about an increasing belief in the soul as a reality independent of the body, immortal and expectant of an afterlife or even rebirth. Plato's philosophy, in its own way, clearly carried forward this concern for the care of the soul.

A number of times in the *Dialogues*, Plato rather casually analogizes Socrates's philosophical enterprise to a mystery cult, with references to the Lesser and Greater Mysteries of Eleusis, the ecstasy of the Korybantes, Bacchic enthusiasm, and so on. Actually, the structure of philosophy, as set out in the previous section, can be compared to that of a mystery cult. First comes admission to the cult—in the case of Eleusis, for example, the Lesser Mysteries, which took place in Athens, were undergone only once since they qualified the initiate for all that came after. In philosophy, the equivalent would be the "test" followed by what I have called "commitment." Then comes a stage of instruction, for which the Greek term is *paradosis*; in the Mysteries, this consisted of rituals in which priests transmitted truths, and in many cases, books were read aloud. In the case of Eleusis, these were elaborate Greater Mysteries that could be enjoyed more than once. In philosophy the equivalent is dialectic, the "activity." Finally, there came the achievement of "perfect knowledge"; at Eleusis, this was called *epopteia*, "looking upon"—a term evidently used by many cults for their final stage. The equivalent in philosophy would be the *telos* as discussed above. The top of Diotima's ladder is actually called *epoptika* (*Symposium* 210a).

Walter Burkert (1987, chap. 3) particularly emphasizes the importance of *paradosis*; the mystery cults were in this sense, educational. It seems likely that mystery cults were one model for the institutional development of the philosophical schools. Plato was actually honored as a kind of sacred founder; his grave was in the Academy with an altar beside it, and Speusippus, his successor, told at his funeral banquet the story of how Plato's real father was not Ariston but rather the god Apollo.

None of this appears in the *Letter*. The specifically religious element is represented only on the mythical level. Plato writes (*Letter* 335a):

> We must ever really accept the ancient and sacred stories that inform us that the soul is immortal and comes before its judges and pays the greatest penalties when it is done with the body. This is what forces us to believe about the greatest wrongs and crimes that it is a lesser evil to suffer them than to commit them.

These sentences are part of Plato's counsel to the friends of Dion; they are, however, not phrased as advice but as something they must believe, that is, as dogma. Unquestionably, Plato believed that the proper care of the soul, involving abstinence both from excessive pleasures and evil acts, led to a far better life in this world. However, he knew too well the power of temptations and the fear that might make us yield to the unjust. Therefore he asserts the necessity of a transcendent reward for justice in the next life, where all the wrongs against the just will be righted by the punishment of the unjust.

In Plato's *Dialogues*, this doctrine is represented in the modality of myth: in the *Crito* (54b–d), in the *Apology* (41a), in the *Phaedo* (107c–108c), in the *Gorgias* (523a–525c), in the *Republic* (614c), and in the *Laws* (905a–b). Plato's Socrates, of course, tells many other mythical stories, but this myth of judgment, rewards, and penalties after death, is the most pervasive. The *Letter* singles it out as the one necessary doctrine and therefore presents the speaker not only as a dialectical teacher but as a prophet—not only Parmenides but also Empedocles. He incorporates in his philosophy an element of West-Greek theology: the souls shall be judged, rewarded, or punished either in their next earthly life when reborn, as in Empedocles, or in their condition in the afterlife, as in Pindar's Sicilian odes, or both, as in Plato's Myth of Er.

We shall never know to what degree Plato himself believed in the literal truth of this doctrine. It may be that Socrates in the *Phaedo* speaks for Plato when he concludes his telling of the myth (114d–115a):

> To claim that things are exactly as I have told them is unfitting for a man of sense, but that something like this is true of our souls and their dwellings, if the soul does turn out to be immortal, that seems to me fitting and a chance worth taking by one who thinks these things are so—it is the best kind of risk—and this incantation he must say over and over to himself—which is why I made so long a myth; these are the reasons for good hope concerning his own soul when a man in his life has banished those other pleasures and ornaments that have to do with the body—they are externals; he must set to work with the conviction that the other kind are greater, so he focused on learning and so ornamented his soul not with external ornament but with its proper ornament, temperance and justice and courage and liberality and truth, and thus he will be ready for the journey to Hades.

Plato's faith was indeed in Apollo's motto: "Know yourself"—as he understood it. It occurs in the *Letter* as friendship to oneself. Plato's conclusion concerning his adventures in Syracuse, implicit in the *Letter*, is that, while he failed in Syracuse, he did not fail himself. For him, it seems clear this was a religious commitment.

Conclusion

In this account, I have addressed a number of issues. One is Plato's autobiographical account of his adventures. This is not, so far as we can tell, untruthful, but with the aid of other sources, we can see that it is falsified to the degree that it is presented as a one-to-one conflict between Plato and Dionysius. Others were involved, other philosophers, some on Plato's side, such as Xenocrates and Speusippus, and others in opposition, such as Aristippus and Aeschines. Then there was Philistus, the intellectual leader of the anti-Platonic forces, an independent intellectual and a worthy adversary.

There is also Plato's estimation of Dion, which (despite Plato's doubts about his resort to military force) is unreservedly positive. Plato does not like to acknowledge the degree to which Dion's whole policy supported his own struggle for power for himself and his family. Nor does Plato mention the murder of Heracleides, which is the blackest moment in Dion's political history. Not even Dion, evidently, could find his way to regime change without bloodshed.

Plato overall shows himself politically quite innocent; in fact, the whole *Letter* is a protestation of innocence. He admits that he made mistakes—most obviously in returning to Dionysius's court when there was nothing for him to do there—but protests that his motives were good and his expectations not unreasonable. As to the latter, we may question his judgment, as to the former, suspect his grandiosity.

Here, I have tried to suggest the historical context—the political developments that led Plato to the notion of the philosopher-king—and then to show how ill-adapted this notion was to realities. I have not, however, tried to explain Plato's turn to philosophy; this aspect of his biography remains obscure. (Acquaintance with Socrates is not a sufficient explanation; the majority of those who knew Socrates—taking the list of those present at his death—had no tendency toward philosophical careers.) Throughout Plato's work, whatever the question, philosophy is the answer; however, there is nowhere a clear statement of philosophy, of what it consists. In the *Apology*, it apparently consists of moral exhortation; in the *Republic*, it is a certain kind of argument that leads to the establishment of sound and stable first principles. Neither account of philosophy occurs in the *Letter*, although, as usual, philosophy is the answer: it is the reliable source of virtue and happiness. The *Letter*, however, adds something nowhere else explicit in Plato: that philosophy cannot be put into words, that it is a kind of discourse founded on friendly contention, culminating in a kind of enlightenment, something very simple, inexplicable, and unforgettable, which makes all the difference. This, it seems, cannot be acquired from books but must be transmitted from soul to soul. If you wanted to know Plato's philosophy, you had to go and talk with him—or with another such person, if you could find one. And this talk would be effective only if prolonged.

Then, in the *Letter*, there is an assertion of the one indispensable myth: the judgment of the soul after death and reward or retribution. That alone, it seems, secures the whole process of the care of the soul: from ascetic commitment, through dialectical disputation, to achieved enlightenment. It might be asked whether a way of life that requires the support of a myth thereby, to some degree, confesses its own weakness.

Even if the *Letter* is not by Plato, it deserves our respect as a representation of his personality and commitments and as an account of his philosophical activity. Even if not true, it is *ben trovato* and can be the foundation for entertaining certain hypotheses about the meaning of his life and works. It therefore challenges us to reread his *Dialogues*. Everything in them is from him, not only Socrates but also his adversaries. The *Dialogues* are the way we have Plato, but on the evidence of the *Phaedrus* and the *Letter*, they were not so important to him. More important was the Academy, along with it there was his hope that philosophy would reform the world. That this last proved a forlorn hope may, in fact, be the *Letter*'s most important lesson. In Syracuse, it seems Plato learned that the kind of trust and friendship philosophy requires can be achieved only somewhere sheltered from the world: this space, Plato's Academy, turned out to be the nascent model developed by the Lycaeum, the Stoa, and Epicurus's Garden. These were the founding institutions of our tradition of higher education.

APPENDIX

A Translation of Selections from Plutarch's *Life of Dion*

3: As the elder Dionysius took command, he immediately married the daughter of Hermocrates of Syracuse. This woman—as the tyranny was not yet firmly established—was subjected by some in the Syracusan resistance to outrages against her person so dreadful and obscene that she voluntarily took her own life. Once Dionysius had secured command and achieved power, he married again: two women simultaneously, one from the Locrians named Doris, the other Aristomache, a local girl, daughter of Hipparinus—the leading citizen of Syracuse, joint ruler with Dionysius when the latter was chosen general with sole authority in military matters.

We are told that he married them both on the same day, and no person knew with which wife he first consorted; thereafter he spent time with each in equal shares; they became accustomed to eating meals together with him; night by night, they took their shares of sleeping with him.

The fact is the people of Syracuse wanted the native-born to have more than the stranger, although the latter, bearing the eldest son of Dionysius herself, assured the security of his kinship. Aristomache lived childless with Dionysius, although he made a point of her pregnancy—he actually accused the Locrian's mother of poisoning Aristomache and had her executed.

4. The brother of that wife was Dion; to start with he was honored because of his sister, later on as he gave evidence of his intelligence, he became on his own a favorite of the tyrant—who instructed all his other stewards to give Dion whatever he asked for, telling him what was given the same day. As he was basically of a proud disposition, generous and manly, he developed further in this direction: by some divine chance Plato landed in Sicily—this was not arranged by any person. Rather some supernatural actor, as it seems, aiming at the far-off liberty of Syracuse and contriving the fall of the tyranny, brought Plato from Italy to Syracuse and introduced Dion into his conversation. Dion was then

very young, the most teachable of all Plato's companions and the most apt for teaching as to virtue, as Plato himself has written and the events bore witness. He had actually been raised by the tyrant as a submissive person, to an unsteady and perilous way of life, a parvenu lifestyle of vulgar luxury; as a consumer of pleasures, thinking excess to be nobility, he became used to it and stuffed with it, yet when he first heard the discourse of a philosophy leading the way to virtue, his soul was swiftly ignited; furthermore, he expected, in his youth and innocence, from his own responsiveness to the best that Dionysius would be responsive to the same discourse, so he focused on managing to create an occasion where he could meet Plato and hear him.

5. Their conversation when it happened was all about virtue—with, however, the greatest difficulties concerning courage since Plato showed that no one is less courageous than tyrants; from this he turned to an exposition of justice, that the happy person is among the just, whereas the life of the unjust is miserable; the tyrant would not put up with such doctrines; he felt he was being tested; he became enraged with the audience, in that they were astonishingly influenced by this man and enchanted by his arguments. Finally, angry and exasperated, he asked him: "What were you after that brought you to Sicily?" He answered that he was seeking a good man. "Well, by the gods," he said, "obviously you haven't found anyone like that." At that, Dion's people thought this would not be the end of his anger; they hurried to put Plato on board a trireme in which Pollis the Spartan was bound for Greece.

Dionysius made a secret request of Pollis that, preferably, he should kill the man on the voyage or at least sell him as a slave. This would not harm him at all since he would continue to be happy being just, even though he'd be a slave. We are told that for this reason, Pollis taking him to Aegina sold Plato into slavery. At that time they were at war with Athens and there was a decree that any Athenian captured in Aegina should be put on the market.

However, Dion in the sight of Dionysius was not diminished in trust or honor; rather he carried through his most important embassies; he was particularly impressive when he went to Carthage. Also, he was nearly the only person allowed freedom of speech, fearlessly stating the facts—as in his rebuke concerning Gelon—because when Gelon's rule was jeered at, and Dionysius himself said that Gelon had become the laughingstock[1] of Sicily, everybody pretended wonder at the gibe, but Dion was disgusted. "Actually," he said, "you were trusted with a tyranny because of Gelon, but no one else will be so trusted because of you"—because Gelon really put on the finest performance of a city ruled by a single man, while Dionysius put on the ugliest.

* * *

10. So Dion, seeing, as we are told, [the young Dionysus] damaged by lack of education and corrupted in habits, invited him to turn toward education and to entreat with every kind of entreaty that the foremost philosopher should come to Syracuse. Upon his arrival, he would make himself available so that habits could be regulated by discourse into virtue, assimilated to the most divine and fairest model in existence; the universe, following its lead, replaces disorder with order. In this way, great happiness would be secured for himself, great also for his citizens; and though they now dwell in hopelessness given the necessity of rule, all these things would provide temperance and justice with paternalistic kindness, and the tyrant will become a king. Not by those unbreakable bonds which your father claimed as his own, fear and force and a multitude of ships and ten thousand barbarians as his guard, but consensus and morale and the grace afforded by virtue and justice—which things, although gentler than those violent and harsh ways, are more powerful as to the fundamental continuity of government. Apart from these things, that ruler is neither ambitious nor competitive, who, although he's singularly clothed in body, splendid in the delicate decoration of his house and his furniture, nonetheless engages in conversation and discourse no more serious than casual talk, not thinking it necessary that his soul maintains some royal adornment, fit for a king.

11. Dion raised these concerns over and over and interspersed certain of Plato's discourses, until an acute and mad passion seized upon Dionysius for the discourse and company of Plato.

---

1. Dionysius puns on the similarity between the Greek word for laughter (*gelōs*) and Gelon's name.

Immediately many letters from Dionysius to Plato came to Athens, also many inquiries from Dion, with others from Italy from the Pythagoreans exhorting him to take hold of the young soul led astray by great authority and power, and master him with weighty discourse.

So Plato, as he himself admits, mainly being ashamed of himself lest he should seem to be mere talk, unwilling to take in hand any action, also anticipating that by purifying a single man in charge, he could heal all Sicily of her disease, consented.

The people opposed to Dion, afraid that Dionysius might convert, persuaded him to call back from exile Philistus, a man cultivated in discourse and also completely familiar with the ways of tyrants, thinking to have him as an adversary to Plato and philosophy.

Philistus actually showed himself completely loyal to the tyranny from the time of its installation and for a long time defended the fortress on the acropolis as the garrison commander.

There was a story that he had an affair with the mother of the elder Dionysius, of which the tyrant was not completely ignorant. Since Leptines, who had two daughters by a woman he had successfully seduced while she was living with another man, gave one of them to Philistus, not telling anything to Dionysius, the latter, enraged, confined the woman in fetters and expelled Philistus as an exile from Sicily to certain connections of his up the Adriatic, where it seems he had the leisure to complete the greater part of his *History*. He did not return during the lifetime of the elder Dionysius, but after the latter's death, as was said, the hostility of others to Dion brought him back, thinking that he would be useful to them and completely loyal to the tyranny.

12. Well, this man as soon as he came back identified with the tyranny. It so happened that there were others who made slanders and accusations to the tyrant against Dion that he had been discussing the dissolution of the regime in favor of Theodotus and in favor of Heracleides. He actually hoped, most likely, that Plato's presence would alter the absolute despotism of the tyranny and establish Dionysius as some kind of moderate and lawful ruler. If he would go against him and would not soften, he planned to dismiss him and turn the constitution over to the Syracusans, not that he favored democracy, but that he thought it altogether superior to tyranny for those who fell short of a healthy aristocracy.

13. When matters were in such a state, Plato arrived in Sicily; in their first meeting, he met with wonderful affection and respect. An impressively decorated royal chariot was waiting when he got off the trireme, and the tyrant made sacrifice in thanks for the great good fortune which had come to his rule. The restraint of his banquets and the decorum of his court, along with the tyrant's own gentle way of doing business, stirred in the citizens wonderful hopes of change. There was a kind of general rush toward discourse and philosophy, and they say the tyrant's palace was full of dust from the number of people drawing geometric diagrams. Within a few days there was a traditional festival in the palace—and when the herald made the usual prayer that the tyranny should endure many years unshaken, Dionysius, who was present, said (we are told), "Won't you leave off cursing us?" This produced plenty of distress in the party of Philistus; they thought that with time and familiarity, Plato's power would become unbeatable if on such brief acquaintance the young ruler's judgment could be so altered and transformed.

14. So their denunciation of Dion was no longer sporadic and secretive, but out in the open; they said Dion couldn't get away with bewitching and poisoning Dionysius with Plato's discourse so that Dionysius would voluntarily abdicate and Dion, picking up the power he laid down, would confer it on Aristomache's sons, his nephews. Some made a point of their disgust if the Athenians, sailing here with a great force on land and sea, had lost it and perished before they took Syracuse, while now these people would depose Dionysius's tyranny by means of a single sophist, conspiring to persuade him to run from his massive bodyguard and his four hundred triremes and his thousands of cavalry and his many times as many heavy-armed men, so that he would seek out some secret good in the Academy and find happiness in geometry, yielding the happiness of power and money and luxury to Dion and his nephews.

As this, beginning with suspicion, was growing into open wrath and faction, a secret letter was brought to Dionysius which Dion had written to the Carthaginian agents, instructing them, when they were in talks with Dionysius concerning the peace, not to make contact without him, because through him they could make everything permanently binding. Dionysius read this letter to Philistus, and taking Philistus's advice, as Timaeus says, Dionysius beguiled Dion with false words of compromise. He made a pretense of a moderate settlement and said he was merely inviting him from the acropolis to the seaside; then he showed him the letter and accused him of conspiring with the Carthaginians against him. Dion wanted to defend himself but was not heard; rather, just as he was, he was immediately put in a small boat; the sailors were ordered to take him away and land him somewhere in Italy.

15. As this happened, people thought this harsh and there was grief in the tyrant's household among the women. The city of Syracuse was excited, expecting revolutionary events and a quick regime change resulting from the tumult about Dion and the tyrant's general unreliability. Dionysius was aware of this and frightened; he reassured Dion's friends and the women that Dion was not in exile but had just gone abroad, so that he [Dionysius] should not be forced by Dion's presence to act mistakenly through anger at his arrogance. He handed over two ships to Dion's household, telling them to load in whatever of his property they wanted and to send his servants to Dion in the Peloponnese. Dion's property was great, and his lavish furniture and tableware almost on a tyrannical scale; all this his friends collected and sent. Lots more was sent by his women and his followers, enough to make him famous in Greece for his possessions and wealth, so that the affluence of his exile should reflect the power of the tyrant.

16. Dionysius immediately transferred Plato to the acropolis, thus contriving an honorable confinement disguised as kindly hospitality, so that he would not sail off and testify to the injustice suffered by Dion. In time and by shared conditions of life, like an animal stroked by a man, he became accustomed to putting up with Plato's company and his discourse; he fell in love with a tyrannic sort of love: he thought he alone was worthy to be loved in return by Plato, and to be most wondered at of any, since he was ready to turn over his affairs and the tyranny if only he would not value Dion's friendship more than his own.

For Plato this condition of his was a misfortune; Dionysius was crazy with jealousy like people unlucky in love, falling into many rages with him in quick succession, with as many reconciliations with entreaties that he could listen to his discourse and share his philosophical activity—seriously, to the last degree—then he was ashamed before those who rejected him, like it would be the death of him.

In the midst of this, a certain war broke out, so he sent Plato away, promising that in a certain season of the year he would send for Dion. This promise he immediately broke, but he did send the income from his properties, thinking that Plato would be understanding about the delay because of the war (for when there was peace, he would right away send for Dion), so he was counting on him to keep quiet and not to stir up trouble or bad-mouth him to the Greeks.

17. Plato tried to bring these things about, and once he'd turned him toward philosophy, included Dion in the Academy. He resided, however, with Callippus, one of the members.

He acquired a farm as a recreation, and later when he sailed for Sicily, he gave it to Speusippus as a gift. Speusippus was his best friend in Athens; he dined with him—since Plato wished that through enjoyable company, finding opportunities for modest playfulness, Dion's character would be tinctured with a sense of the pleasurable. Speusippus was just the man for that: Timon in Silloi calls him "good at jokes."

When Plato was assigned to pay for a boy's chorus, Dion took responsibility for the chorus and covered the whole cost out of his pocket. Plato approved of Dion's seeking public recognition in this way; Plato was more concerned about Dion's being seen favorably than about his own reputation.

Dion went about to the various cities; he relaxed with the best people, the political leaders, and joined their collective rituals, displaying nothing awkward or tyrannical or dissolute in his manners but rather good sense and virtue and courage, graceful in his conversation as to his discourse and his philosophy. In this way he acquired general goodwill and admiration, along with public honors and civic decrees. The Lacedaemonians made him a Spartan citizen, disregarding the anger of Dionysius—even though Dionysius was their faithful ally against the Thebans.

We are told that Dion was once invited to the home of Ptoeodorus of Megara. Evidently Ptoeodorus was a rich and powerful person. When Dion saw a crowd around his doors, a mass of busy people, and that Ptoeodorus was difficult to access and unavailable to them, he glanced at his friends, who were disapproving and annoyed and said, "Do we find fault with this? Because we ourselves always did such things in Syracuse."

18. In the course of time, Dionysius, becoming jealous and fearing the favorable opinions gained by Dion among the Greeks, stopped sending his revenues and handed the property over to handpicked trustees. In his wish to fend off any ill repute due to Plato among the philosophers, he gathered together many people noted for their education. As he was ambitious to excel everyone in dialectic, he was compelled to misuse certain misunderstandings of Plato. So then he longed for him again and decided it was his own fault that he had not made the best use of him when he was around, nor had he heard all he had on offer. In the way of a tyrant swept away by his desires and instantly eager, so he went after Plato using every trick in the book. He persuaded the Pythagoreans around Archytas to invite Plato as guarantors of the agreements. It was through him that alliance and guest-friendship first occurred between them. They sent Archedemus to bring him. Dionysius sent a trireme and friends who should invite Plato. He himself wrote a clear and plain letter, saying that nothing owed to Dion would be returned if Plato did not consent to come to Sicily, but if he consented, everything. Many considerations came to Dion from his sister and wife, pleading that Plato consent to Dionysius and make no excuse. Thus Plato says that he came for the third time to the strait by Scylla,

> "So that he should still measure out dread Charybdis."

19. When he arrived there was great joy, with great hope for Sicily, that joined in prayer and mutual effort, Plato could overcome Philistus, and philosophy, tyranny.

The women paid special attention to him, also Dionysius showed him a special trust shown no one else: he could approach him without a body-search.

There were many and various gifts of money—some offered, others refused —Aristippus of Cyrene was there and remarked that Dionysius's generosity played it safe: he offered them small gifts when they asked for large ones, while he offered much to Plato, who wouldn't take it.

After the opening greetings, Plato broached the topic of Dion. There were at first delays, then complaints and quarrels unnoticed by outsiders—they were concealed by Dionysius, who attempted with various services and marks of respect to distract Plato from his favorable view of Dion—Plato however from the very beginning did not reveal his own distrust of him and his lies, but rather carried on and pretended otherwise. These then were their mutual relations, which they thought others failed to notice.

Then Helikon of Cyzikus, one of Plato's followers, predicted an eclipse of the sun; when it happened as he foretold, the tyrant, impressed, presented him with a talent of silver. Aristippus, joking with the other philosophers, said he also could predict an unexpected event. When they asked him to tell it, he said: "I foretell that quite soon Plato and Dionysius will be enemies." As it turned out, Dionysius sold Dion's property and kept the money. Plato moved into the palace garden and lived with the mercenaries. They had hated him and wanted to kill him, thinking that he was trying to persuade Dionysius to give up the tyranny and live without a palace guard.

20. When Plato was in such danger, Archytas's people learned of it and promptly sent ambassadors and a galley, asking Dionysius for the man and saying that he had taken them as guarantors of safe passage when he sailed to Sicily. Dionysius apologized for the hostility with feasting and greetings for the party, and even said this to him: "Well, Plato, I suppose you'll have some harsh accusations of us with your philosophical friends." He smiled and answered: "We don't have such a shortage of topics in the Academy that we'll remember you." This, they say, was Plato's answer, but it doesn't actually sound like Plato himself.

BIBLIOGRAPHY

Primary Texts

Archytas. *Fragments*. In *Archytas of Tarentum: Pythagorean, Philosopher, and Mathematician King*, edition, commentary, and introduction by C. A. Huffman Cambridge University Press, 2005.

Aristophanes. *Acharnians*. In *Aristophanes Comoediae*, vol. 2, edited by F. W. Hall and W. M. Geldart. Clarendon Press, 1907.

Aristophanes. *Lysistrata*. In *Aristophanes Comoediae*, vol. 2, edited by F. W. Hall and W. M. Geldart. Clarendon Press, 1907.

Aristotle. *De arte poetica*. Edited by R. Kassel. Clarendon Press, 1965.

Aristotle. *Fragmenta selecta*. Edited by W. D. Ross. Clarendon Press, 1955.

Aristotle. *Ethica Nicomachea*. Edited by J. Bywater. Clarendon Press, 1894 (Reprinted 1962).

Aristotle. *Mechanica*. Edited by O. Apelt. Leipzig, 1888.[1]

Aristotle. *Politica*. Edited by W. D. Ross. Clarendon Press, 1957.

Aristoxenus. *Die Schule des Aristoteles: Texte und Kommentar*. 2nd ed., Vol. 2, *Aristoxenos*, edited with commentary by F. Wehrli. Benno Schwabe & Co., 1967.

Cornelius Nepos. "Life of Dion." In *Cornelii Nepotis Vitae cum fragmentis*, edited by P. K. Marshall. Teubner, 1977.

Diodorus Siculus. *Bibliotheca historica*. In *Diodorus of Sicily in Twelve Volumes*, edited by F. R. Walton, translated by C. H. Oldfather. Vols. 5 & 6. Harvard University Press, 1950/1954.

Diogenes Laertius. *Lives of the Eminent Philosophers*, edited with an introduction by T. Dorandi. Cambridge University Press, 2013.

Homer. *The Iliad*. Translated by A. T. Murray. Revised by William F. Wyatt. 2 vols. Harvard University Press, 1924.

Homer. *The Odyssey*. Translated by A. T. Murray. Revised by George E. Dimock. 2 vols. Harvard University Press, 1919.

Inscriptiones graecae IV[2]. *Inscriptiones Argolidis, 1, Inscriptiones Epidauri*. Edited by Friedrich Hiller von Gaertringen, Berlin-Brandenburgischen Akademie der Wissenschaften 1929.

Ion of Chios. *Fragments*. In *Die Fragmente der Vorsokratiker*, 6th ed., edited by H. Diels. Weidmann, 1951 (Reprinted 2004).

---

1. This work is generally considered to be spurious.

Plato's Seventh Letter

Isocrates. *Isocrates.* Edited and translated by G. Norlin. 2 vols. Harvard University Press, 1980.
Lysias. *Lysias.* Edited by W. R. M. Lamb. Harvard University Press, 1930.
Plato. *Platonis Opera.* Edited by John Burnet. 5 vols. Oxford University Press, 1900–1907.
Plutarch. *Life of Dion.* Edited by W. H. Porter. Hodges, Figgis, and Co., 1952.
Thucydides. *Historiae.* Edited by H. S. Jones and E. Powell. Clarendon Press, 1942.
(Pseudo-) Xenophon. *Constitution of the Athenians.* In *Xenophontis opera omnia*, vol. 5. Clarendon Press, 1920 (Reprinted 1969).
Xenophon. *Hellenica.* In *Xenophontis opera omnia*, vol. 1. Clarendon Press, 1900. Reprinted 1968.
Xenophon. *Memorabilia.* In *Xenophontis opera omnia*, 2nd ed., vol. 2. Clarendon Press, 1921. Reprinted 1971.

Secondary Literature

Allen, D. *Why Plato Wrote.* Wiley-Blackwell, 2010.
Andrewes, A. "The Arginousai Trial." *Phoenix* 28 (1974): 112–22.
Berve, H. *Dion.* Steiner, 1957.
Brisson, L. "La Lettre VII de Platon, une autobiographie?" In *L'Invention de l'autobiographie d'Hésiode à saint Augustin*, edited by Marie-Françoise Baslez et al. Éditions Rue d'Ulm, (1993) 2018. https://doi.org/10.4000/books.editionsulm.6377.
Brunt, P. A. "Plato's Academy and Politics." In *Studies in Greek History and Thought*. Oxford University Press, 1993.
Burkert, W. *Lore and Science in Ancient Pythagoreanism.* Harvard University Press, 1972.
Burkert, W. *Ancient Mystery Cults.* Harvard University Press, 1987.
Burnyeat M., and M. Frede. *The Pseudo-Platonic Seventh Letter*, edited by D. Scott. Oxford University Press, 2015.
Caven, B. *Dionysius I: Warlord of Sicily.* Yale University Press, 1990.
Davies, J. K. *Athenian Propertied Families 600–300 BC.* Clarendon Press, 1971.
Dornseiff, F. "Platon's Buch 'Briefe.'" *Hermes* 69 (1934): 223–26.
Edelstein, L. *Plato's Seventh Letter.* Brill, 1966.
Finley, M. I. with Smith, D. M. *A History of Sicily*, abridged and revised by Christopher Duggan. Viking, 1987.
Helfer, A. *Plato's Letters: The Political Challenges of the Philosophic Life.* Cornell University Press, 2023.
Huffman, C. *Archytas of Tarentum: Pythagorean, Philosopher, and Mathematician King.* Cambridge University Press, 2005.
Irwin, T. "The Inside Story of the Seventh Platonic Letter: A Sceptical Introduction." *Rhizai: A Journal for Ancient Philosophy and Science* 2 (2009): 127–60.
Knab, R. *Platons Siebter Brief.* Georg Olms Verlag, 2006.

Liatsi, M. *Die semiotische Erkenntnistheorie Platons im Siebten Brief: Eine Einführung in den sogenannten philosophischen Exkurs.* C. H. Beck, 2008.

Lombardini, J. *Plato's Political Thought.* Brill, 2023.

Maddalena, A. *Platone: Lettere.* Laterza, 1948.

Mele, A. *Taranto dal IV secolo a.c. alla conquista romana.* In *Taranto e il Mediterraneo: atti del quarantunesimo Convegno di Studi sulla Magna Grecia, Taranto 12–16 ottobre 2001*. Istituto per la Storia e l'Archeologia della Magna Grecia, 2002.

Metcalf, R. "Plato's Discovery in Sicily: Philosophy and Life-Structuring Practices in the Seventh Letter." In *Plato at Syracuse: Essays on Plato in Western Greece with a New Translation of the Seventh Letter by Jonah Radding*, edited by H. L. Reid and M. Ralkowski. Parnassus Press, 2019.

Nails, D. *The People of Plato: A Prosopography of Plato and Other Socratics.* Hackett Publishing Company, 2002.

Notomi, N. "Plato, Isocrates and Epistolary Literature: Reconsidering the Seventh Letter in its contexts." *Plato Journal* 23 (2022): 67–79.

Parente, I. M. *Filosofia e politica nelle lettere di Platone.* Guida, 1970.

Pasquali, G. *Le lettere di Platoni.* Le Monnier, 1938.

Politis, V. "Plato's Seventh Letter: A Close and Dispassionate Reading of the Philosophical Section." *Classics Ireland* 27 (2020): 56–77.

Reale, G. *Zu einer neuen Interpretation Platons: Eine Auslegung der Metaphysik der großen Dialoge im Lichte der „ungeschriebenen Lehren."* Translated by Ludger Hölscher. Ferdinand Schöningh, 1993.

Redfield, J. *The Locrian Maidens: Love and Death in Greek Italy.* Princeton University Press, 2003.

Reid, H., and Ralkowski, M. *Plato at Syracuse: Essays on Plato in Western Greece with a New Translation of the Seventh Letter by Jonah Radding.* Parnassos Press, 2019.

Riedwig, C. *Pythagoras: His Life, Teaching, and Influence.* Cornell University Press, 2005.

Romm, J. *Plato and the Tyrant: The Fall of Greece's Greatest Dynasty and the Making of a Philosophic Masterpiece.* W.W. Norton & Company, 2025.

Sanders, L. *The Legend of Dion.* Edgar Kent, 2008.

Sayre, K. M. "Plato's Dialogues in Light of the *Seventh Letter*." In *Platonic Writings, Platonic Readings*, edited by C. L. Griswold Jr. Routledge, 1988.

Schneider, M. T. "Success Against All Odds, Failure Against All Logic: Plutarch on Dion, Timoleon, and the Liberation of Sicily." In *Plato at Syracuse: Essays on Plato in Western Greece with a New Translation of the Seventh Letter by Jonah Radding*, edited by H. L. Reid and M. Ralkowski. Parnassus Press, 2019.

Todd, S. C. *The Shape of Athenian Law.* Clarendon Press, 1993.

Von Fritz, K. *Platon in Sizilien und das Problem der Philosophenherrschaft.* De Gruyter, 1968.

Waterfield, R. *Plato of Athens: A Life in Philosophy.* Oxford University Press, 2023.

Westlake, H. D. "Dion and Timoleon." In *The Cambridge Ancient History*, vol. 6. Cambridge University Press, 1994.